C000258135

The
HORNCASTLE
AND
TATTERSHALL
CANAL

by
J.N. Clarke

THE OAKWOOD PRESS

© Oakwood Press 1990

ISBN 0 85361 398 2

Typeset by Gem Publishing Company, Brightwell, Wallingford, Oxfordshire.

Printed by Alpha Print, Witney, Oxfordshire.

Sir Joseph Banks Baronet, President of the Royal Society.

(Etching published by H. Colburn & Co. August 1820 — original loaned by Horncastle Local History Society.)

Sir Joseph Banks was the original sponsor of the Horncastle Canal project, Chairman of the Steering Committee, and during difficult times was responsible, by his financial support, for seeing the work through to completion.

He was lessee of the Manor of Horncastle from the Bishop of Carlisle, and owned and leased a large acreage of land through which the canal passed. Sir Joseph was also a Drainage Commissioner, and after his return from a South Sea voyage as botanist with Captain Cook in 1768 he set in hand drainage works in Horncastle and the town's ancient manorial allotments in Wildmore Fen. His country seat was at Revesby Abbey near Horncastle, and he erected a large town house in Horncastle.

Published by
The OAKWOOD PRESS
P.O.Box 122, Headington, Oxford.

Contents

HORNCASTLE NAVIGATION.

CAUTION TO BOATMEN.

WHEREAS much injury has been caused to the works of this Navigation by persons in charge of Boats drawing the top cloughs of the locks, and so flushing their boats through the locks instead of drawing them out with their hauling lines:

ALSO by drawing the cloughs without first closing the bottom doors of the locks:

ALSO by putting ropes round the Jack heads and balance beams of the locks, instead of round the posts on the lock sides provided for the purpose:

ALSO by striking their boat hooks into the lock doors.

NOTICE IS HEREBY GIVEN, that the above practices will not be allowed, nor flushing of any kind, and that all persons found offending will be proceeded against for the penalties provided by the Act.

BY ORDER,

RICHD. & ROBT. CLITHEROW,

CLERK.

Sir Joseph Banks' town house was the building with the name W. Bryant showing; the frontage faced High Street. The Midland Bank building on the right of the Market Place (between Morton and Salter & Salter) was erected on the site of the home of Richard Clitherow, Clerk & Treasurer to the Horncastle Navigation Company. The memorial on the left is in memory of Edward Stanhope of Revesby Abbey who received the estate from J.B. Stanhope to whom it was left by Sir Joseph Banks.

A fine view of the towpath near the South Basin.

Foreword

At the end of the eighteenth century the market town of Horncastle which received its charter from Henry III in 1231, had a population of less than 2,000, housed mainly in mud-and-stud cottages. The Parish Vestry controlled the common lands which were still farmed on the open field system.

Owing to lack of communications there was little or no trade outlet except by trains of packhorses or stage wagons over often unpassable roads. Thus trading was confined to the catchment area of approximately 40 villages within a radius of from 6 to 8 miles – the distance it was possible for villagers to ride or walk to market and return home the same day.

Within 10 years the situation had changed completely, due mainly to the initiative and continued drive of one man — Sir Joseph Banks of Revesby Abbey. By 1793 work on construction of a canal linking Horncastle with the River Witham at Tattershall had commenced. In 1802 the canal was open to traffic along its entire length, and by 1805 the town's open fields had been enclosed, thus releasing land for house building and industrial development. The number of households rose rapidly from 382 in 1792 to 571 in 1811, and during the same short period the population rose from 1,834 to 2,622. The canal was the catalyst which brought about that development of Horncastle from a somewhat sleepy rural service centre into a thriving Victorian market town with a wide range of crafts, light industry, and trade. The canal has had brief mentions in various books and magazines, but a full account of its construction and working has not been previously attempted. I hope this study will adequately fill that gap in local history, and at the same time give pleasure to readers.

I am indebted to the staff of Lincolnshire Archives Office and Lincoln City Reference Library for their help and facilities; to the Queen's Champion Lt Col J.L.M. Dymoke M.B.E., D.L., of Scrivelsby Court for access to family papers; to Mr David Boulton of Horncastle for a number of relative references from the Stamford Mercury newspaper. Also to Mr B. Benson-Brown of High Toynton for photograph and information on the Dunham & Pollexfen firm of Wool Merchants. Over many years the late Mr Richard Chatterton, Mr E.C. Peacock, and Mr Reginald Tweed, Solicitors of Horncastle allowed me access to Petty Sessions Minute Books, and documents relative to the Horncastle Navigation Company and Horncastle Railway, and their kindness is remembered. Many of those documents are now deposited in the Lincolnshire Archives Office and will come under their copyright. I have therefore quoted L.A.O. references where appropriate, and appreciate permission to reproduce. Mrs C.M. Wilson, Assistant Director Museums, Lincoln County Council, and Mr R. Clapson of Barton-on-Humber have been helpful in suggesting sources for information on boats. Dr W.M. Hunt of Boston College kindly allowed me to quote from his Ph.D. treatise on 'The Role of Sir Joseph Banks in Promoting Lincolnshire Navigations and Canals' deposited in the Lincolnshire Central Reference Library at Lincoln.

I would also like to thank Mr J.C. Porter of Tattershall, Mr B. Hipkin of Coningsby, Mr F. Bailey of Tattershall, Mr W. Johnson and Miss Pearl

Wheatley of Horncastle, all of whom have helped with photographs, and the staff of Horncastle County Library for their courtesy and help over the years.

Of particular help has been the interest shown in the book by Mr Dave Carnell, Chairman of the Lincolnshire and South Humberside branch of the Inland Waterways Association, East Midlands Region.

Detailed references and other acknowledgements, also an index, are included at the back of the book.

J. Norman Clarke
Belchford 1989

Note: All photographs, unless credited individually, are from the author's collection.

Mason's Bridge Coningsby, adjacent to an old ford. This bridge was of a much stronger construction than those shown in the other illustrations.

Other works by J.N. Clarke:

Chapter One
Why Construct a Canal?

Before the beginning of the 19th century the growth and prosperity of Horncastle, as indeed most market towns, had always been limited by lack of sufficient transport and efficient communications with the outside world. There were large surpluses of hides from tanners, and corn and wool from surrounding farms, which merchants in Horncastle could only distribute to larger markets and manufacturing towns by means of packhorses or slow lumbering wagons, drawn by teams of horses over roads or tracks so bad as to be impassable for many months of the year. For instance when Bishop Wake travelled from Horncastle to Boston in 1709 his coach overturned in the middle of a slough of mud, and he had to continue his journey on horseback.[1] For heavily laden wagons such a road would have been impassable. The importation of salt, coal and other heavy goods such as iron for blacksmiths and wheelwrights was equally difficult. The type of wagon then in use can be seen in some of the paintings by Peter de Wint and W. Callow in the Usher Art Gallery at Lincoln.

From the last decade of the 18th century onwards into the first quarter of the 19th century, enclosure of the open fields and resultant improvement in farming methods brought about a steady increase in wool and corn production on the Lincolnshire Wolds, and this increased distribution problems and inhibited business for the corn and wool merchants in Horncastle. There were only two toll roads from Horncastle at that time, both in a northerly direction, one to Louth and the other to Lincoln. The Horncastle–Lincoln Turnpike was set up under Acts of 1759, 1780 and 1806, and the Horncastle–Louth Turnpike under an Act of 1773.[2]

Farmers not only needed an outlet for their products, but if they were to exploit their land to its full potential they needed lime and organic manures such as bonemeal, dried blood, cake and cattle feed in large quantities. There was thus a two-way transport problem inhibiting the development of agriculture and trade in the eastern area of south-east Lindsey.

An additional problem was that much of the land south of Horncastle was very low-lying and subject to flooding. Improved drainage was, therefore, necessary either through a deepening of the bed of the River Bain, or canalising it via a series of locks and staunches.

Some heavy goods and produce had come to Horncastle via the River Witham in the 17th and 18th centuries. In 1719 the Lord of the Manor of Kirkstead claimed a toll of four pence for each load of goods landed at Kirkstead Wath, and a merchant from Lincoln objected because he had always previously sent his goods to Horncastle Fairs by water carriage to Kirkstead where they were landed without tolls, and then carried by land to Horncastle.[3] A canal connecting the River Witham to Horncastle was an obvious step in the development of communications and trade for the town and surrounding villages.

Fortunately for Horncastle and district Sir Joseph Banks (1744–1820) had inherited a large estate at Revesby, and was also lessee of the Manor of

Horncastle from the Bishop of Carlisle, thus he had strong local interests in agriculture and trade. He was a dominant personality in the County as well as on the national scene, being a J.P., personal friend of the King, Fellow of the Royal Society, and a skilled botanist, so having influence in London as well as locally. By 1790 he was already considering sponsoring an Enclosure Act for Horncastle and the drainage of Wildmore Fen, and saw the desirability of canalising the River Bain from Horncastle down to the River Witham. Once Sir Joseph Banks gave his support to a project it was not long before progress was made, and as will be seen it was undoubtedly his interest which saw through the completion of the Horncastle Canal. The Enclosure Act for Horncastle and Wildmore Fen was passed in 1801, and the Award made in 1805.[4]

Sir Joseph's enthusiasm was not without personal interest, because he had large landholdings in many of the parishes in the River Bain catchment area. The Horncastle Enclosure Award alone allocated him 145 acres as his personal allotment, in addition to that made to him as Lessee of the Manor of Horncastle.

Although the two largest contributors as shareholders in the canal project were Sir Joseph Banks and Lord Fortescue, there were 294 other initial shareholders under the Act of 1792 coming from a wide cross section of the population, so making it a locally financed enterprise (*see Appendix Three*).

Copy of a draft of a public notice which proves the canal was open throughout its length in 1875.

Chapter Two

The Water Sources Available and Early Developments

The primary essential for a canal is, of course, a sufficient and preferably steady supply of water available throughout the year, and the Rivers Bain and Waring, both of which flow into Horncastle and join to form one stream south of the town, appeared at first sight to be ideal for the purpose.

The River Bain like most of the Wold streams was formed originally by glacial meltwater. It rises west of Ludford, flowing southwards along 22 miles through Horncastle to the River Witham near Tattershall. The River Waring rises from springs on Ings Farm, Belchford five miles north-east of Horncastle. It is joined by Park Drain in the middle of the village, and then flows south to join the River Bain in Horncastle where a tongue of gravel separates the two rivers at their confluence, and on that tongue of gravel the town of Horncastle developed.[5]

Unfortunately the water flow in both rivers has always been erratic. The Bain has a long and wide catchment area, and in times of heavy rain quickly reaches flood level. The Waring normally has a very slow flow, but just north of Horncastle it is joined by a small stream, The Thunker or Scrafield Beck, which in heavy rains has a very fast flow of water. In the 19th century the stream drove a watermill which powered a brass foundry. The water-wheel had a diameter of 12 ft and carried 26 buckets. Conversely both rivers during the summer have very little flow, and due to the shallow depth of water are liable to freeze over during hard winters.

Except in times of flood, retention of sufficient water in the canal would always be a problem and would need close watch by the staunch keepers and careful use of the locks by boatmen. As will be seen later, the boatmen often emptied whole lengths of the canal by their carelessness.

There was always another factor to keep under consideration, namely the height of the River Witham at Tattershall, which affected the efficient working of the final locks.

From the above details, the reader will not be surprised that the erratic water supply caused problems throughout the lifetime of the canal.

The land marked 'Part of Thornton' on the Plan of 1819 is liable to flooding. At some time, probably in the 17th century, the River Bain was extended and looped in order to take a water supply to the tanners on the south side of West Street (formerly Tan & Far Street).

The North Ings Drain, South Ings Drain, and Staunch were constructed on orders of the Enclosure Commissioners in 1805 in an effort to avoid flooding. They are shown on the map at p.38. The course of the rivers Bain and Waring are clearly shown on the Plan of 1819, on which is shown the Dry Dock built by the Navigation Company.

In 1791 Sir Joseph Banks contacted landowners who owned estates along the banks of the River Bain south of Horncastle, also local business and

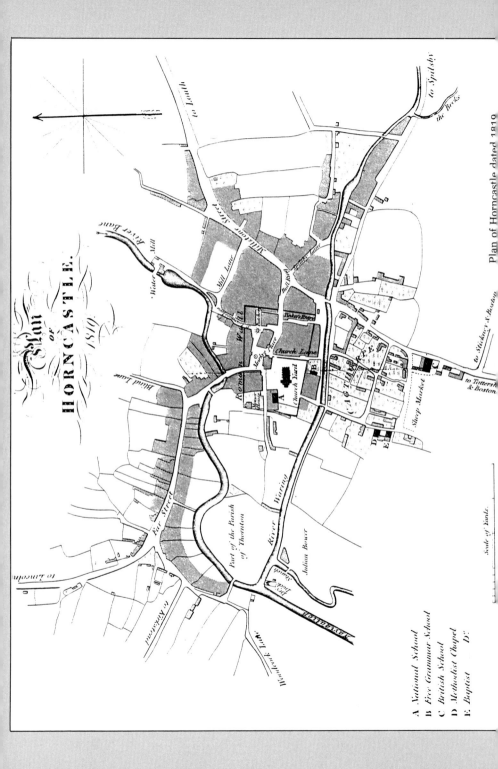

Plan of Horncastle dated 1819

A *National School*
B *Free Grammar School*
C *British School*
D *Methodist Chapel*
E *Baptist Dᵒ*

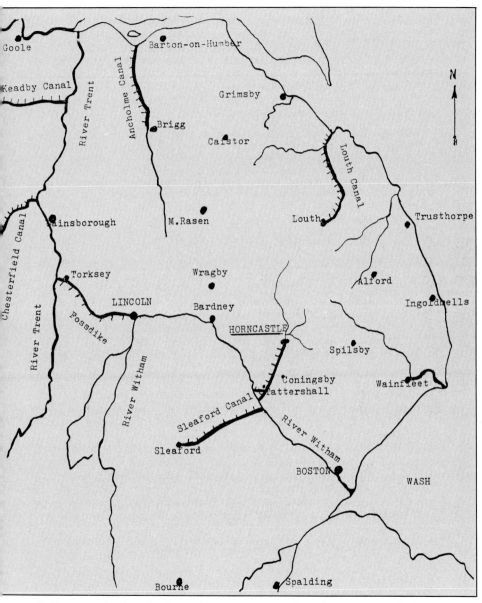

A diagrammatic plan showing main watercourses and canals in East Lincolnshire, and Horncastle's links with Boston, Lincoln and the Midlands — from Horncastle to River Witham — Lincoln via Bardney Lock — Brayford — Fossdyke Canal — through Torksey Lock on to River Trent — Gainsborough, Newark, Nottingham — the Midlands were then accessible from the River Trent through a number of links such as the Chesterfield Canal, and Stainforth and Keadby Canal, the Calder and Hebble, and the Leeds and Liverpool canals.

professional men, and solicited their support for the construction of a canal between Horncastle and the River Witham. An unofficial steering committee was formed, a preliminary survey of possible routes was commissioned, and Robert Clitherow, a Horncastle solicitor who acted for Sir Joseph in local matters relating to his Revesby Estate, was asked to arrange for the drafting of a Parliamentary Bill.

By March 1792 a draft Bill was ready for consideration by the committee, and an advertisement was placed in the *Stamford Mercury* newspaper inviting all interested persons to a meeting:

30th March, 1792. *Horncastle Intended Navigation.*
Notice is hereby given that a General Meeting of all persons interested in this Navigation and also the improvement of the navigable communication through the City of Lincoln, is requested at the Bull Inn in Horncastle aforesaid, on Wednesday the 4th Day of April next at ten of the clock in the forenoon to hear the Bill read, and finally to settle the several clauses therein, and transact such other business as may be necessary.
By order of the Committee,
Richard Clitherow, Solicitor.
Horncastle 19th March, 1792.

Progress was rapid. The draft Bill was approved and presented to Parliament. It became law on 11th June, 1792 (32 George III cap. 107, 1792) authorising the formation of the Company of Proprietors of the Horncastle Navigation in the County of Lincoln. As will be seen from the copy of the first page of the Act, this sets out the intentions of the legislation, and the first two pages of the preamble includes a complete list of the original petitioners and sponsors.

The company was granted perpetual succession and a Common Seal, and was empowered to raise £15,000 in shares not exceeding £50 in value. No person was to possess less than one whole share or hold more than 20. Interest was to be limited to eight per cent. If necessary the company was authorised to raise an additional sum of £10,000 by mortgaging the tolls. The Act also authorised purchase of the existing Tattershall Canal (Gibson Cut) for the sum of £840.

The Tattershall Canal had been constructed in 1786. It consisted of a short length of canal, about one mile, with one lock, from the River Witham near Tattershall Ferry to the village of Tattershall near the Market Place and Castle. The canal had been constructed by John Gibson of Tattershall and John Dyson of Bawtry, both general merchants, but John Dyson had some engineering experience and he helped in construction of part of the Sleaford Canal.

When the share certificates began to be issued it became necessary for the Navigation Company to have a Common Seal. The committee, as usual showing deference to Sir Joseph Banks, asked him to submit a design, which he did. Eventually after two other designs had been considered unsuitable, the one shown on the title page was accepted by the committee. It is not clear who actually designed it. The motto *Auspicium melioris aevi* roughly translates as 'Omen of a better age', or in more basic English 'The hope of better things to come'. The steel die for the Seal cost 12 guineas.[6]

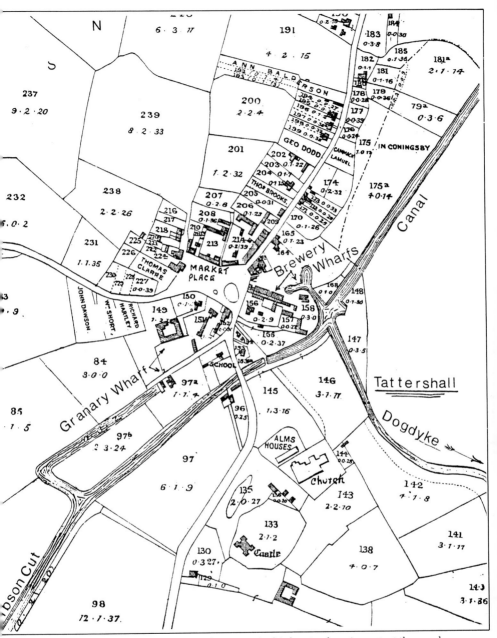

An estate plan dated 1867 (scale 6 chains = 1 inch) showing how important the canal had been to Tattershall. The feeder arm from the Gibson Cut led to Granary Row where there was a wharf on which were built substantial corn warehouses. Just past the confluence of the Gibson Cut and Dogdyke section of the canal another feeder can be seen, leading to two basins where wharfs housed malt kilns, brewery warehouses and brewery, and coal yards. All the wharfs were situated almost in the centre of the village near the market place.   *Plan kindly loaned by Mr J.G. Porter of Tattershall*

The canal, sometimes referred to as the Gibson Cut, had been constructed on land leased to them by Lord Fortescue who held the Lordship of the Manor of Tattershall. Gibson and Dyson did not obtain an Act of Parliament as was usually the case for canal works, and it is interesting that Lord Fortescue should allow the project to go ahead on his land without Parliamentary approval. The Horncastle Act of 1792 made that lease null and void, but laid down that Lord Fortescue was to be recompensed for loss of the lease by the Horncastle Navigation Company to which the land was to be transferred.

When the Tattershall Canal had been constructed Gibson and Dyson had erected a large warehouse at the Tattershall end near the market place, part of which warehouse stretched over the end of the canal. The warehouse was excluded from the sale, but Gibson and Dyson had to take down that portion of the warehouse which protruded over the canal, and build a higher arched road bridge over the canal, which the Navigation Company were to extend to the River Bain.

In addition to local supporters of the Horncastle Navigation, the petition to Parliament for the Act was sponsored by Lincoln and Boston Corporations, the members of which obviously saw the possibilities of increased trade from Horncastle and its catchment area of villages. The channel under Lincoln High Bridge was too shallow to allow vessels through into the Brayford, so they had to be off-loaded and the goods taken by road the short distance to the Brayford. Here they were loaded on to other vessels before the cargo could be taken further along the Fossdyke to Torksey, and then on to the River Trent to the Midlands. The channel under the bridge was deepened in 1797 to 3 ft 6 in., and this was in no small measure due to the initiative of Sir Joseph Banks who pressed for a relevant clause to be inserted in the Horncastle Bill with the agreement of Lincoln Corporation, and Witham Navigation Commissioners. The clause stated that the Witham Navigation Commissioners, Horncastle Navigation Company and Sleaford Navigation Company were to share the cost between them. There was later some dispute about payment, but eventually the Horncastle Navigation Company paid their contribution which amounted to £1,165.

The Act gave the Horncastle Navigation Company complete and absolute control over its watercourses:

> The Horncastle Navigation or any works to be made by virtue of the said Act shall not be subject to the control, direction, survey or order of any Commission of Sewers.

On the suggestion of Sir Joseph Banks, the Engineer William Jessop was consulted about the survey which had been made, and after consideration he recommended two alternative plans for construction of the canal, which included purchase and incorporation of the existing Tattershall Canal into the schemes.

The first proposal was to make a completely new canal cut across country from Horncastle to Kirkstead, estimated to cost £12,544. One of the main problems with that scheme was that it would mean constructing at least 22 bridges at a cost of £1,650 and the Navigation Company would be respon-

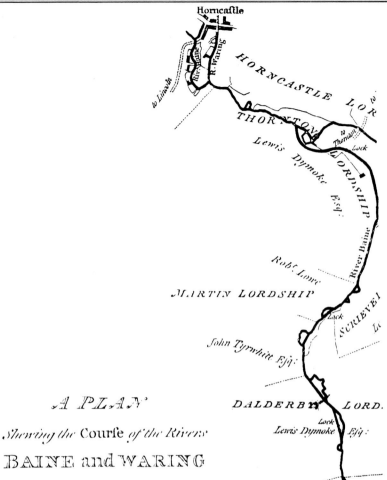

Horncastle

R. Waring

to Lincoln

HORNCASTLE LOR

THORNTON LORDSHIP

to Thornton

Lock

Lewis Dymoke Esq.

River Baine

Robt. Lowe

MARTIN LORDSHIP

SCRIEVEL

Lock

John Tyrwhit Esq.

DALDERBY LORD.

Lock

Lewis Dymoke Esq.

A PLAN

Shewing the Course *of the Rivers*

BAINE and WARING

and the Works proposed to be executed thereon,

to open a Navigation from

HORNCASTLE *to the* RIVER WITHAM

in the

County of Lincoln.

Surveyed by

Robt. Stickney and Saml. Dickinson,

1792.

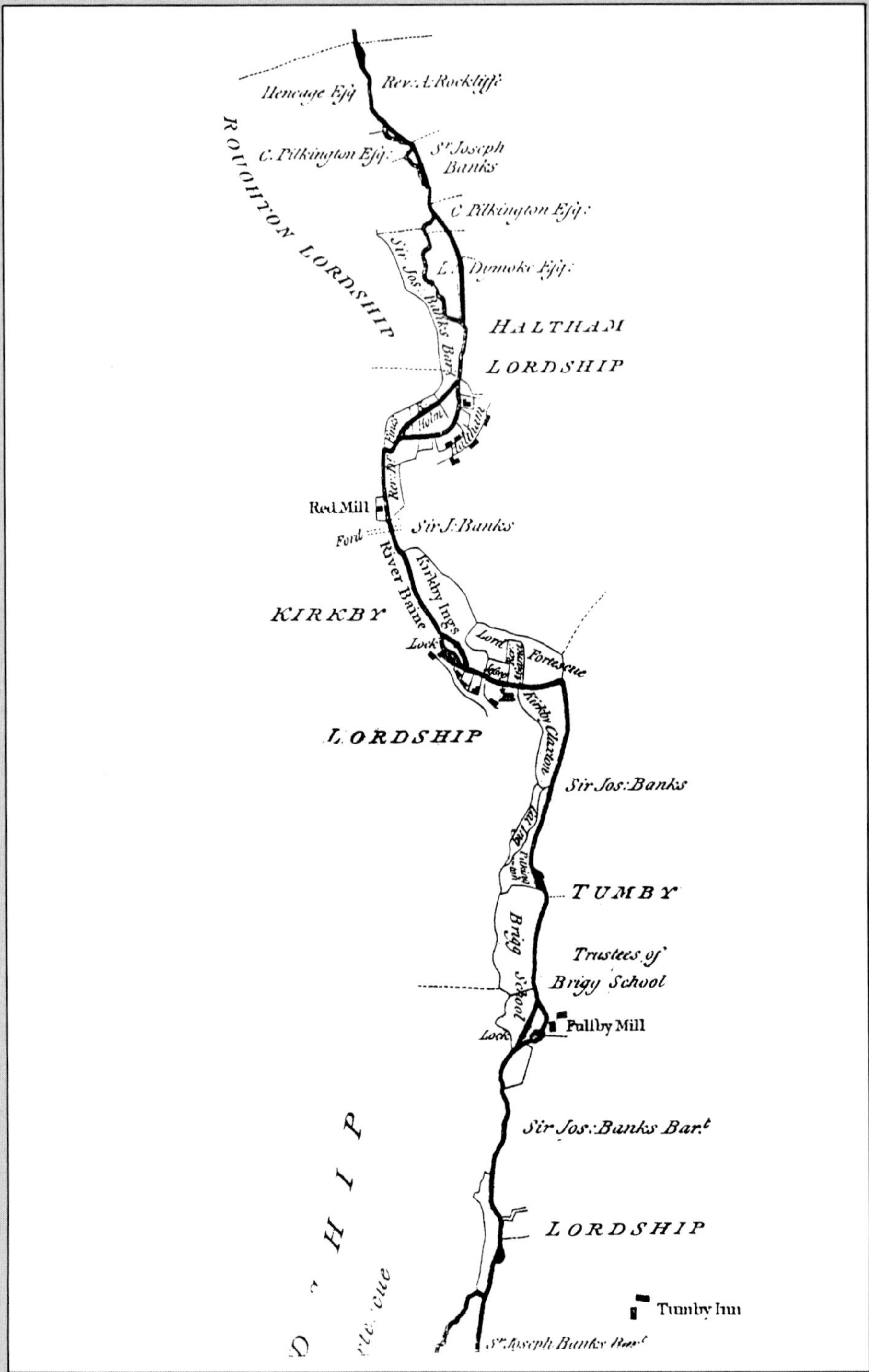

Rev. A. Rockliff

Heneage Esq.

ROUGHTON LORDSHIP

C. Pilkington Esq.

S.r Joseph Banks

C. Pilkington Esq.

L. Dymoke Esq.

S.r Jos. Banks Bank

HALTHAM

LORDSHIP

Holme

Haltham

Red Mill

Ford

S.r J. Banks

River Bain

Kirkby Ings

KIRKBY

Lock

Lord Fortescue

LORDSHIP

Kirkby Clawson

Sir Jos. Banks

TUMBY

Brigg School

Trustees of
Brigg School

Lock

Fulsby Mill

Sir Jos. Banks Bar.t

LORDSHIP

Tumby Inn

S.r Joseph Banks Bar.t

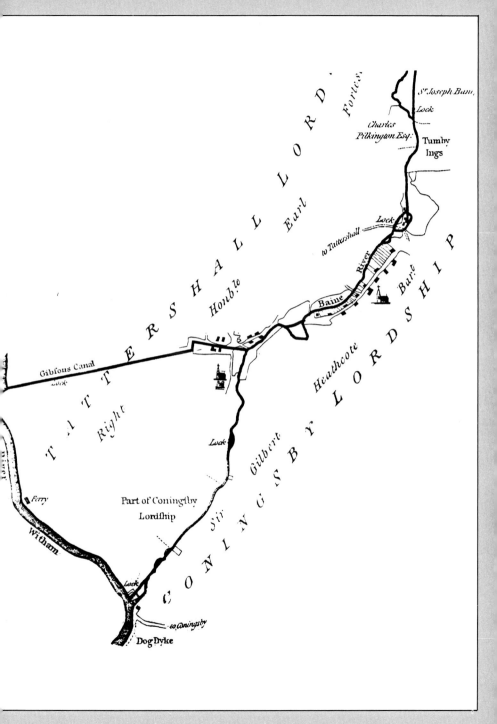

ANNO TRICESIMO SECUNDO

Georgii III. Regis.

* *

C A P. CVII.

An Act for enlarging and improving the Canal
called *Tatterfhall* Canal, from the River
Witham to the Town of *Tatterfhall*, and extending the fame into the River *Bain*, and
for making the faid River *Bain* navigable
from thence to or into the Town of *Horncaftle*, all in the County of *Lincoln* ; and
alfo for amending and rendering complete
the Navigable Communication between the
faid River *Witham* and the *Fofdyke* Canal,
through the *High Bridge*, in the City of
Lincoln.

ꟺꞪꝐꞅꝐꞅ

The first page of the Horncastle Navigation Act 1792.

3044   ANNO REGNI TRICESIMO SECUNDO Cap. 107.

Preamble.

WHEREAS the enlarging and improving a certain Canal lately made by John Gibson of Tattershall, in the County of Lincoln, Merchant, and John Dyson of Bawtry, in the County of York, Merchant, from the River Witham, near a Place called Tattershall Ferry, in the Parish of Tattershall aforesaid, to the Town of Tattershall, and extending the same into the River Bain, within the said Parish of Tattershall; and also the making and maintaining the said River Bain navigable from thence to or into the Town of Horncastle, all in the said County of Lincoln, through the several Parishes or Townships of Tattershall, Coningsby, Tattershall Thorpe, Tumby, Kirkby on the Bain, Haltham on the Bain, Roughton, Dalderly, Martin, Scrielsby, Thornton, and Horncastle, will open a Communication with the Port of Boston, and the City of Lincoln, whereby the Carriage of Coals, Corn, Wool, Lime, and other Goods and Merchandize, will be greatly facilitated at much less Expence than is now paid for the same by Land Carriage, not only to the Advantage of the said City, and the Towns of Boston, Horncastle, and Tattershall, but of the Inhabitants of the large Tract of Country adjacent to the said Rivers, and be of publick Utility: And whereas the several Persons herein-after named are desirous, at their own proper Costs and Charges, to make and maintain the said Navigation, but cannot effect the same without the Aid and Authority of Parliament: May it therefore please Your Majesty that it may be enacted; and be it enacted by the King's most Excellent Majesty, by and with the Advice and Consent of the Lords Spiritual and Temporal, and Commons, in this present Parliament assembled, and

Proprietors.
by the Authority of the same, That William Charles Allenby, Daniel Allenby, Sir Joseph Banks Baronet, Samuel Barnard, William Barton, William Bell, John Betts, the Mayor and Corporation of Boston, Messieurs Boyers and Harrison, Robert Broughton, John Brumhead, Patrick Cawdron, Thomas Cheyney, John Chislett, Richard Clitherow, James Conington, the Honourable Champion

Pages from Act of 1792 authorising establishment of the Company of Proprietors of the Horncastle Navigation, including names of the first sponsors and shareholders.

Dymoke, the Reverend John Dymoke, Richard Ellison, Richard Ellison junior, William Elmhirst, the Reverend John Fret-
well, Thomas Fydell, Messieurs Garfit and Claypon, John
Grant, Messieurs Gee and Clarke, Ann Goodwin, Edward
Harrison, Thomas Hawling, John Hill, Robert Kelham,
John Loder, Griggs Lunn, Phillippa Massingberd, Eliza-
beth Massingberd, the Reverend William Massingberd, Joseph Newbound, Titus Overton, John Overton, John
Parkinson, Cooke Richardson, William Robinson, Messieurs Sheath and Squire, Messieurs Sheath and Wray,
Abraham Sheath, John Short, William Hirst Simpson,
Charles Southby, Francis Thirkill, the Reverend William
Tyler, William Walker, Thomas and Samuel Waite, and
their several and respective Successors, Executors, Admi-
nistrators, and Assigns, together with such other Person
or Persons as shall at any Time hereafter be possessed of
One or more Share or Shares, as herein-after mentioned, of the said Navigation, are and shall be united
into a Company for the better carrying on, making, and
maintaining the said Navigation, and for making, erecting,
and maintaining Towing Paths, Dams, Locks, and Cuts,
and for building Toll Houses and other Conveniencies
near any such Locks, and for making, completing, and
maintaining all such other Works as may be necessary
for the said Navigation, according to the Rules, Orders,
and Directions, herein-after expressed, and shall for that
Purpose be one Body Politick and Corporate, by the
Name of The Company of Proprietors of the Horncastle *Incorporated.*
Navigation, in the County of Lincoln, and by that Name
shall have perpetual Succession and a. Common Seal,
and by that Name shall and may sue and be sued, and
also shall and may have Power and Authority to purchase
Lands, to them, and their Successors and Assigns, for
the Use of the said Navigation only, without incurring
any of the Penalties and Forfeitures of the Statutes
of Mortmain, or any of them, and also to sell any of the
Lands or Tenements purchased for the Use of the said
Navigation; and any Person or Persons, or Bodies
Politick, Corporate or Collegiate, may give, grant,
bargain, sell, or convey to the said Company of Proprietors, any Lands, Tenements, or Hereditaments, for the

(14)

ESTIMATE of the Expence of making NAVIGABLE the RIVER BAINE, for VESSELS of 54 Feet in Length, 14 Feet 4 Inches in Width, and drawing 3 Feet 6 Inches of Water.

	£.	s.	d.
WIDENING, deepening, and ſtraightening the River, ſo as to be 18 feet wide at the bottom, 30 feet wide at the top, and 4 feet deep, with the neceſſary Cuts and deviations	2,438	0	8
12 Locks, at £420 each	5,040	0	0
8 Flood-ſluices, at £70 each	560	0	0
12 Bridges, at £80 each	960	0	1
Walling of two Baſons at *Horncaſtle*	180	0	0
Purchaſe of 30 Acres of Land, £40 per Acre	1,200	0	0
Clearing the Works of Water during the Execution,	400	0	0
Two Miles of Fencing, at £66 per Mile	132	0	0
Gates and Drop-ſtiles in the croſs Fences	100	0	0
Gravelling the Haling-path	120	0	0
Contingencies at £10 per Cent	1103	0	0
£	12233	0	0

W. JESSOP

(15)

ESTIMATE of the Expence of a CANAL from HORNCASTLE to KIRKSTEAD for VESSELS of the ſame Dimenſions as above.

	£.	s.	d
CUTTING the Canal to an 18 feet bottom, with ſlopes of 18 Inches to a foot, ſo as to make it 30 feet wide at the top water, and 4 feet in depth	2,464	0	0
Extra cutting through high Ground, and banking	250	0	0
Extra Expence of lining the Canal through the leaky Soil	450	0	0
12 Locks at £ 400 each	4,800	0	0
22 Bridges at an average of £75 each	1,650	0	0
Culverts and Overfalls	90	0	0
8 Miles of Fencing	330	0	0
Gravelling the Bank for the Towing-path	240	0	0
Walling the Baſons at *Horncaſtle*	180	0	0
25 Acres of Land through the Incloſures at £ 30 per Acre	750	0	0
20 Acres on the Moor at £ 10 per Acre	200	0	0
Contingencies at 10 per Cent	1,140	0	0
£	12,544	0	0

Newark June 30th. 1791.

W. JESSOP

William Jessop's two alternative plan costings for construction of the Horncastle Canal. The Haling Path was the Towpath.
L.C.R.L. L.386

sible for any repairs. The second suggestion was to deepen the bed of the River Bain, and widen and straighten it where necessary through 11 miles to Tattershall and then to Dogdyke at a cost of £12,233. Twelve locks were proposed in each case to cope with a fall of 84 ft between Horncastle and the River Witham, the locks to be of a size to take vessels of 54 ft × 14 ft 4 in. with a 3 ft 6 in. draught. After consideration of both schemes it was finally decided to proceed with Jessop's preference to canalise the River Bain, but events proved that this decision would have to be partly modified later on. The locks were in fact built to larger measurements (see Appendix Two) and were thus capable of accommodating vessels operating to the Midlands and Yorkshire via the Rivers Witham and Trent.

In his report William Jessop gave as his reasons for preferring the canalisation of the Bain:

> It would take less quantity of water from mills; would be unencumbered with a less number of bridges; and would accommodate a greater number of villages in its route.

He also pointed out that a completely new cut through fresh soil would mean that the banks and bed of such a canal would need puddling along the entire length to avoid seepage of water.

The first actual construction works were carried out on the Gibson Cut, when the existing lock was dismantled and a new one erected, also the canal extended under the road bridge through to the River Bain. The proposed works were advertised in the *Stamford Mercury*[7]:

> Horncastle Navigation.
> The Committee of the Company of Proprietors of the Horncastle Navigation in the County of Lincoln do hereby give notice that they will be ready at the next meeting which will be held at the Bull Hotel Horncastle on Tuesday the 28th August instant at 10 o'clock in the forenoon to receive proposals for the taking up a lock which now stands in the canal leading from the River Witham to Tattershall, and for erecting another lock upon the same canal nearer to the town of Tattershall aforesaid; and also for the widening and deepening the same canal from the said River Witham up to the said town of Tattershall.
> Richard Clitherow
> Clerk to the Company.
> 13th August, 1792.

The first meeting of the company shareholders had been held at the Bull Hotel, Horncastle on 14th June, 1792 when Richard Clitherow a local solicitor was appointed Clerk to the Navigation Company at a salary of £5 5s. 0d. per annum 'to be reviewed at a later date'.[8]

Clitherow was also appointed Treasurer, although there were doubts in the minds of some members whether the joint appointment was prudent. However, the joint appointment was confirmed when Sir Joseph Banks gave his support.

There is undoubtedly substance in Dr W.M. Hunt's opinion that much of the subsequent financial trouble would have been avoided if a separate treasurer *with banking experience* had been appointed, and he suggests Sir Joseph should have used his influence to insist on it.

It is only fair to point out, however, that there were no merchant banks in Horncastle at that time, the first one being established in 1819 — Claypon, Garfit & Claypon, Waterside, Horncastle (drawing on Masterson & Company), Agent Richard Babington. Later, in 1833, the Lincoln & Lindsey Banking Co. came to the Corn Market, Horncastle. The former is now Lloyds Bank, and the latter Midland Bank. It would not really have been practicable with the travel difficulties of 1792 in mind, to have appointed a treasurer from a bank in Lincoln, Boston or Louth.

A separate appointment of treasurer could have been made from another firm of Horncastle solicitors such as Henry Selwood, but probably Sir Joseph was reluctant to incur extra expense. The point must also be made that Clitherow received scant support from shareholders when he called on them to pay their instalments on their uptake of shares, and also when he tried to raise further capital in 1800.

At a meeting on the 27th November, 1792 the question of brick supplies for locks, bridges, staunches and weirs was raised. A survey of suitable sites of clay near the canal had already been made, and on recommendation of the committee it was decided that the bricks were to be 10 in. long by 3 in. deep by 5 in. wide. It is not clear from the Minutes why the advice of an engineer does not appear to have been taken.

The survey had shown suitable clay land near Fulsby Mill; Kirkby North Field between the mill and Red Mill; Roughton Gate; Toft Hill; south end of Roughton town; and below Tattershall. The specification for making the bricks was as follows:

> Digging Clay, giving it three turns, making, burning and delivering good hard merchantable bricks made in a mould 10 inches long 3 inches deep and 5 inches wide.

Tenders were accepted as follows in the sum of 18 shillings per thousand bricks:

> Thomas Dawson site Toft Hill — 100,000 bricks
> Thomas Dawson site Tattershall — 600,000 bricks
> John Rogerson of Tattershall site Fulsby Mill — 200,000 bricks
> John Rogerson of Tattershall site Tattershall — 600,000 bricks
> Joseph Dalton of Swinup(?) site Kirkby North Field — 600,000 bricks.

After tests on bricks fired from the above clay two of the sites appeared to be unsatisfactory, and one different site was chosen at Youl Dales in Coningsby where 1,200,000 bricks were to be made by the above mentioned three brickmakers. After a short time, however, the bricks made by Dalton and Rogerson were not passed by the Engineer, and their contracts were terminated. Thomas Dawson was retained as contract brickmaker to the Navigation, and was given an order for 1,200,000 bricks.[9]

Advertisements for supplies of other goods were placed in the *Stamford Mercury*:

> January 4th 1793. Horncastle Navigation. Oak Timber.
> Whereas a large quantity of Oak Scantlings, of different dimensions will be wanted for the Locks to be built on this Navigation early in Spring; Notice is given that all

No. *244*

COMPANY of PROPRIETORS of the HORNCASTLE
NAVIGATION, in the COUNTY of LINCOLN.

THESE are to Certify, That *William Thirst*
Simpson of Horncastle Mercer

is a Proprietor of One, three hundredth Share of the *Horncaſtle*
Navigation, being No. *244* ſubject to the raiſing more Shares of
Fifty Pounds each, not exceeding the Sum of Ten Thouſand
Pounds in ſuch additional Shares, and to the Rules, Regulations,
and Orders of The ſaid Company; and that the ſaid *William*
Thirst Simpson his

Executors, Adminiſtrators and Aſſigns, is and are entitled to the
Profits and Advantages of ſuch Share.

       GIVEN under the Common Seal of the ſaid Company,
the *Thirst*   Day of *July*
in the Year of our Lord One thouſand Seven hundred
and ninety-five .

Entered
R. Clitherow

Share certificate dated 1795.

persons desirous to furnish the whole, or any part thereof, are requested to deliver their lowest tender per foot solid at or before the next meeting of the Committee which will be held on Tuesday the 22nd January next, and in the meantime the different sizes of scantlings and quantity of each may be known by applying to the Clerk, or to Mr William Walker in Horncastle. By Order of the Committee, Rd. Clitherow.

The William Walker mentioned in the advertisement was a shareholder in the canal company. He was looked upon by the Committee as their un-official expert to keep an eye on things generally as work on the canal proceeded.

A later issue of the paper advertised for craftsmen and workmen:[10]

April 5th 1793. Horncastle Navigation.
A number of brickmakers, brick layers, carpenters, and labourers may have con-stant employment on the above Navigation, by applying to Mr William Cawley Engineer, at the Queen's Head in Horncastle, and who will let all or any part of the works on the same Navigation.

As will be seen from the latter advertisement Mr William Cawley the Engineer had set up office at the Queen's Head Inn (now the Farmers Club) in Horncastle Market Place, and was authorised to take on workmen of various trades.

A few weeks later the Clerk asked shareholders for a further payment on their shareholdings to enable payments to be made for wages and materials.[11]

July 5th 1793. Horncastle Navigation.
The several subscribers to and Proprietors of this Navigation are requested to pay into the hands of the Treasurer £30 per cent of their respective subscriptions on or before the 12th day of August next towards defraying the expense of carrying on the works of the said Navigation, being the third call for that purpose.

The appointment of an Engineer for construction of the canal was for some time in confusion. It had been suggested that the Sleaford and Horncastle Navigation Companies should jointly appoint an Engineer to oversee work on both canals, but Sleaford Navigation Co. started work before an appoint-ment was made.

It needed Sir Joseph Banks to instill a sense of urgency into the project otherwise work would not have started on the main canal when it did in April 1793. The above-mentioned William Cawley of Mickle Trafford in Cheshire was appointed on 5th April, 1793 as the first Engineer at a salary of £300 per annum. He seems to have been something of a 'Hobson's Choice'. The appointment was made only after lengthy correspondence between Sir Joseph Banks and William Jessop, and between the latter and various engineers who showed little or no interest in accepting the job.

The relationship between Sir Joseph Banks and Jessop was more than a little strained over the appointment. Early in 1793 Sir Joseph wrote to Jessop informing him he expected him either to supervise the works himself, or recommend a suitable person to do so. Jessop replied he was under no such obligation, but would endeavour to find some competent engineer to fill the vacancy. Eventually he suggested William Cawley. Jessop made the point that he had set out sufficiently detailed plans from which any competent engineer should be able to complete the work.[12]

The committee thought the salary of £300 per annum was too high, but Sir Joseph pointed out that due to the 'canal madness' there was an acute shortage of engineers with canal experience, and the longer they waited the higher the salary they might have to pay in order to secure someone. As usual his advice was taken and the committee confirmed the appointment. Both the latter and Banks were soon to regret that decision.

On its first test when filled with water the lower lock at Tattershall collapsed, and poor workmanship on weirs and bridges showed that supervision by Cawley had been inadequate. There were other shortcomings, and Cawley was dismissed in October 1793, only six months after starting work on the canal. Amongst reasons given for his dismissal were the following:

> Locks and weirs blowing; buying timber at very high rates when cheaper was available; of overstocking on materials; using wrong lime in construction of weirs which were also made too narrow; using different sizes of bricks; failing to obtain receipts for payment, and failing to keep proper accounts.

There can be no doubt that if the initial works had been well constructed many of the later troubles would not have occurred, the canal would have been completed at least a year earlier, and the cost would have been much nearer the original estimate.

HARRISON's WHARF,

St. KATHERINE'S LONDON.

THE VESSEL NOW ON TURN, TAKING   IN GOODS AT THIS WHARF

For Boston, Lincoln, Horncastle, &c.

Is the *Horncastle*   *Fawcett* Master,

Which will clear on Friday and Sail on Saturday the 5 *June* 1847

No Wharfage charged at Boston. Freights, &c., as low as from any other Wharf.

BE CAREFUL TO ORDER YOUR GOODS TO HARRISON'S WHARF.

THOMPSON AND EMMISON, WHARFINGERS, BOSTON,
W. DIXON, AGENT, HORNCASTLE.

Notice advertising the sailing of the general trader *Horncastle* under Captain Fawcett from St Katherine's Dock, London to Horncastle via Boston and Lincoln. W. Dixon listed as Horncastle Agent was William Dixon, local corn and coal merchant, who lived in East Street, Horncastle.

From original kindly loaned by Mr Hare of Bridge Street, Horncastle

High Bridge and 'The Glory Hole' Lincoln. Vessels from Boston and Horncastle had to pass under the bridge to the Brayford Pool and then on to the Fossdyke Canal to connect with the River Trent at Torksey Lock. Before 1797 vessels had to unload their cargo on one side of the bridge, transport it on land to the other side and re-load it, because the depth of water under the bridge was too shallow to take a loaded barge. When the Horncastle Canal Bill was being drafted, Sir Joseph Banks insisted on a clause being inserted which ensured that the depth of water under the bridge would be at least 3 ft 6 in.

The narrow passage on the left at the end of the houses, led by some steps to High Street. The houses were demolished about 1900.

The Minute Books of the company reveal how much the committee depended on Sir Joseph Banks during the early stages of the project. The members were very reluctant to make any major decision without receiving his prior approval, and a number of meetings were adjourned because Sir Joseph could not be present. Cawley was succeeded by John Dyson of Bawtry who had helped in the construction of the Sleaford and Tattershall canals. Dyson was appointed on 13th March, 1794, also at a salary of £300 per annum. He resigned a year later and was succeeded by John Hudson on 5th April, 1795.

An assistant to Cawley, one John Pacy had been appointed at a salary of £150 per annum, and he was kept on as assistant to Dyson, but Pacy was not happy in the work and resigned on his own accord with effect from 24th March, 1794.

The Tattershall Lock, Tumby Lock and Butts Road Bridge in Coningsby which also collapsed were built by John Jagger, William Hargreaves and George Wass. On 23rd April, 1794 they were given the option of rebuilding them or having their contract for other work declared null and void. They agreed to rebuild. As work progressed the sections completed were opened to traffic, and in 1795 the sum of £250 was collected in tolls.[13] However, by then the canal company was already experiencing severe financial problems because of overspending on estimates, and it was urgently necessary to complete the canal as far as Dalderby (2½ miles from Horncastle) in order to raise more money from tolls. The following notice appeared in the *Stamford Mercury*:

April 3rd 1795. Horncastle Navigation.

Hereby give notice that a General Meeting of the Proprietors of the said Navigation will be held at the Bull Inn Horncastle on Monday the 20th April at 10 o'clock in the forenoon to take into consideration the Company's Finances; to determine upon the best mode of raising a further fund for defraying the expenses of the works already finished; for executing those necessary to complete the Navigation to Dalderby Ford as soon as may be; and letting the tolls to that point with the full dues payable. Given under our hands the 17th March 1795. J. Fretwell, W.H. Simpson, J. Conington, Daniel Allenby, Wm. Walker, T. Overton.

The decision to let the tolls was taken in order to reduce staff. They were taken up by Thomas Coltman of Hagnaby Priory, a local Justice of the Peace in January 1796, who made a loan to the Navigation Company, the interest from which was to be his payment for the tolls. The arrangement was short-lived, however, and the company reverted to making their own collection of tolls.

The works on the canal caused problems for millers and farmers. In addition to the watermill in Horncastle situated at the head of the North Basin, there were three other watermills on the canal line, namely at Fulsby (Tumby), Kirkby-on-Bain, and Coningsby. In September 1793 the millers at Fulsby and Kirkby-on-Bain claimed damages after their mills stopped because of loss of water due to canal works. Farmers also complained about losses of crops because of flooding of their lands due to the canal workings. The claims were agreed by the committee. The canal company was often in trouble with the millers for restricting their flow of water, and had to pay compensation. Even as late as 1880 the compensation to millers for stoppage that year was £94 15s. 3d. The millers' claims must have been legitimate because although the committee resisted almost all other claims against them, they usually paid the millers without quibble.[14]

John Hudson resigned as Engineer on 24th November, 1795, and Joseph Kelsey of Haxey was appointed as Overseer at a salary of 15 shillings per week! He was obviously not a trained engineer. The frequent changes of engineers and overseers on the job must have been the main cause of poor workmanship in the early years of the project.

In anticipation of completion of the canal as far as Dalderby a wharf was constructed there, although it was not finished until 1797. An abstract of title[15] shows that land was leased from Lewis Dymoke of Scrivelsby Court, one of the original shareholders in the Navigation Company:

> 5th April 1797. Lewis Dymoke to Proprietors of Horncastle Navigation Canal. A parcel of meadow at Dalderby (1 rood 35 perches) the River East and North, the Navigation North: to make a Wharf, at a Peppercorn rent for 5 years.

Later on the wharf was extended to cover 1 acre, 1 rood, 1 perch. A Wharfinger and Toll Collector was appointed at a salary of £50 per annum plus a rent free cottage which was erected on the site. That was a good wage at the time, but he was, of course, handling large sums of money and overseeing the storage of goods in a barn which was purchased to act as a warehouse.

The Clerk to the Navigation Company was optimistic about the future now a flow of income from tolls allowed him to settle some of the outstanding accounts. Coal was being brought up the canal from Yorkshire, Derbyshire, and Nottinghamshire, and wool and corn exported down. In 1797 he wrote to Sir Joseph Banks,

> Town of Horncastle & whole neighbourhood have for a month past experienced the utility of our Canal by receiving Coals at Dalderby Wharf 6 shillings per chaldron lower than for some years ... that wool, corn and every kind of merchandise is now carried to and from Lincoln one quarter cheaper than has been accustomed ...

But by the time the canal had been completed to Dalderby in the early months of 1797 money had run out, including the extra £10,000 authorised under the Act as mortgage on tolls. For five years, therefore, from 1797 to 1802 Dalderby Wharf served as the terminal of the canal, goods being taken to and from the wharf there for and from Horncastle by road.

On the advice of Sir Joseph Banks the committee decided to ask the well known consultant engineer John Rennie to advise on completion of the canal, and in October 1799 after taking a survey he recommended continuing from Dalderby by a new straight cut west of the River Bain (which he considered much too winding to be of use), the cut to be 30 ft wide and 3½ ft deep, at an estimated cost of £8,291. The works which had already been completed were by then deteriorating, and in parts were in danger of

Dalderby Lock looking north. This was the terminal point of the canal from 1797 to 1802.

Cottage built for Wharfinger and Lock Keeper at Dalderby Wharf.

collapse due to bad weather and flooding, and it was imperative the canal be completed and repairs effected without delay.

In 1800, therefore, the company obtained a further Act (39 & 40 George III cap. 109 9.7.1800) allowing the raising of £20,000 either by subscription amongst existing shareholders, by issue of further shares of £50, by mortgage of tolls, or by granting annuities. There was no limitation under the Act as to the number of shares to be held by one person.[16] Sir Joseph Banks purchased twenty £100 shares, but otherwise very little money was attracted to the scheme from local sources, and in order to complete the work by 1802 the company had, in June 1801, to take up a large mortgage on the tolls amounting to £20,600, the money being supplied by Sir Joseph Banks and Lord Fortescue. This was a bad start to the project, because it meant that nearly all tolls received for the first 20 years were absorbed in paying off the mortgage, the first dividend to shareholders not being issued until 1813. Once the mortgage had been assured a meeting was called to consider tenders for completing the canal, the following advertisement appearing in the *Stamford Mercury* on 10th July, 1801:

HORNCASTLE NAVIGATION.
A meeting of the Committee of the said Navigation Company will be held in the Bull Inn, Horncastle on Tuesday 23rd July to receive proposals from and contracts with such persons as may be willing to execute the works necessary for completing the said navigation from Dalderby Wharf into the town of Horncastle; and that the attendance of such Proprietors to whom it may be convenient is earnestly requested. By order of the Committee Richard Clitherow Clerk and Treasurer. N.B. Plans and specifications of intended Locks can be seen at Mr. Clitherow's office in Horncastle.

On Wednesday 2nd September, 1801 a contract was signed for the above works with Messrs Joseph Myers, Thomas Simpson and John Wilson in the sum of £6,800. The 'Engineer' appointed to supervise the last stage of the work was William Walker mentioned previously. His appointment had been supported by Sir Joseph Banks, but Walker was not a qualified engineer.[17]

John Rennie would not be in charge of the work himself. His involvement like Jessop's ended when his plan and specifications were accepted and his fees paid. The Resident Engineers such as Cawley, Dyson, Hudson and Walker supervised the actual construction, and dealt with the numerous small contractors who carried out the work.

Excavation was carried out by navvies using spades, shovels and barrows. Stonemasons and bricklayers built the locks, bridges and weirs; carpenters and joiners made the huge lock gates, and mud puddlers sealed the sides of the cuttings against leakage. Local labour was used to dig out clay for brickmaking; bankers made up the banks with soil excavated from the cuttings, and consolidated the towpath which was made on one side of the canal only, for horses which pulled the barges. The length of canal under construction at any one time would be a hive of activity. The wharfs and locks were lined with huge blocks of stone, much of it from Derbyshire, linked together in some places by iron dowels or clamps. Mooring rings were set in the stone facings of the wharfs and locks, and bollards erected on the wharfs. Some of the stone was supplied by Tootle and Beaumont of Doncaster. Alder poles and timber were brought from Northamptonshire.[18]

By September 1802 works on the canal were almost completed, and the following notices appeared in the *Stamford Mercury*:[19,20]

> Horncastle Navigation.
> Annual General Meeting 23rd September at 10 am Bull Hotel Horncastle. The works being now nearly completed, the Committee will be glad to see the Proprietors in time to view the works in and near the town before the general business of the day commences.

> Horncastle Navigation.
> Annual General Meeting stands adjourned to 13 October . . . and it appearing that £1000 only is now wanted to complete the works of the said Navigation, Mr Griggs Lunn, one of the Proprietors, hath offered to advance same on the conditions of the last subscription.

Not much is known about the workmen who constructed the canal — navvies or bankers — but they lived rough and sometimes clashed with local villagers. In 1792 the navvies employed in cutting the canal at Tattershall took forcible possession of the village and the Angell Inn (now Fortescue Arms) bringing up beer from the cellars in buckets. Soldiers had to be called in to quell the riot. (*History of Tattershall* by M.A. Pickworth Lincoln 1891.)

Delivery note for 1 hamper for Mr. . . . of Horncastle. The original note was unfortunately damaged by flood. The provenance of the note would suggest the vessel sailed from Thompson & Emmison's Wharf at Boston. The captain's name was Elwiss.

There were dozens of these footbridges over the canal, most of them built to the design shown. According to Jessop's estimates they cost approximately £80 each including materials and erection.

Kirkby-on-Bain near the church.

Tattershall over branch of Gibson Canal.

North basin of canal and wharf: note public pump and watering place for horses, watermill in background. The basin was used for baptisms by Horncastle Baptists in early years of the 19th century. Three boys in the background are fishing.

The staunch (or stanch) was constructed under the Horncastle Enclosure Award of 1805 to control the flow of water in the South Ings Drain, and which affected also the volume of water reaching the canal.

The Stanch, Horncastle.

Chapter Three

Boats using the Horncastle Navigation in the Early Years

Towards the end of the 18th century Parliament passed legislation requiring owners of vessels which sailed on rivers and canals to register their boats, showing details of owner, name of boat, tonnage, crew, type of boat and where the vessel operated. Boats on the River Witham and associated canals were registered in Lincoln, and from the Register (L.A.O. Lincoln Boat Book L/1/5/9) it has been possible to find details of the earliest boats working on the Horncastle Canal. Two of the boats were operating from Dalderby when that hamlet was at the head of the canal before it was completed.

Date	Name of Owner	Name of Boat	Type of Boat	Tonnage	Name of Crew	Where Operating
16. 5.1800	Gilliatt & Wilson, Dalderby	Martha	Ketch	34	John Kirk & 1 helper	Dalderby– Lincoln & Boston
9. 4.1801	J. Cuthill of Lincoln	Betsy	Ketch	35	James Boothby & helper J. Cole	Dalderby– Lincoln & Boston
3. 6.1803	John Wilson & Benjamin Gilyard	Margaret	Sloop	42	John Wilson & helper	Horncastle– Wakefield
10. 6.1803	John Wilson & Benjamin Gilyard	King George	Keel	41	John Kirk & helper W. Musgrave	Wakefield– Horncastle
12. 7.1803	Daniel Boyers Horncastle	Stranger	Sloop	46	Master & one man	Horncastle– Halifax
1. 9.1804	Daniel Boyers Horncastle	British Queen	Keel	41	Thomas Lenton & one man	Horncastle– Lincoln– Boston
24. 4.1805	Ben. & Stephen Scott of Horncastle	Commerce	Keel	45	Jos. Cole & one man	Horncastle– Boston– Wakefield
24. 4.1805	Ben. & Stephen Scott of Horncastle	Hope	Sloop	45	Master & one man	Horncastle– Manchester
17. 5.1805	Benjamin Gilliatt of Horncastle	Maria	Sloop	42	J. Willson & one man	Horncastle– Wakefield
2.10.1807	James Cuthill of Lincoln	Albion	Sloop	46	W. Mills & 1 man & 1 boy	Horncastle– Wakefield

All the above owners were listed as Merchants. James Cuthill of Lincoln owned boats in 1795 trading from Lincoln to Leeds, Hull, Gainsborough and Wakefield. The Gilliatt family carried most of the coal and other goods from Dogdyke station to Horncastle, under contract to the Great Northern Railway in 1852 and 1853, before the railway line was constructed to Horncastle.

John Kirk of Horncastle was running two vessels registered in the town in 1842, carrying coal there from Nottingham, Derbyshire and Shardlow.

The main difference between the various vessels was in their size and rigging of sails rather than the hull shapes. Keels had a single mast and square sail roughly amidships, the sail usually being brown in colour. The sloops had a single mast also, with fore and aft rigging. Ketches were smaller in size with two masts and fore and aft rig. Sloops, keels and ketches were the largest types of vessel to use the Horncastle and Tattershall Canals, but many of the boats would be smaller lighters or barges with no sails, used mainly for journeys along the canal itself. They were, however, clinker built on similar lines to the sloops. A 'general trader' type of vessel carried both people and goods — it was the waterway equivalent of the highway carrier cart or wagon. The term barge was a general term used by local people when referring to most vessels on the canal, although they did usually refer to 'steam packets' as such. Many of the steam packets acted as general traders, or market boats.

Thomas Brewer and Thomas Rushton were also boat owners in Horncastle during the 1840s.

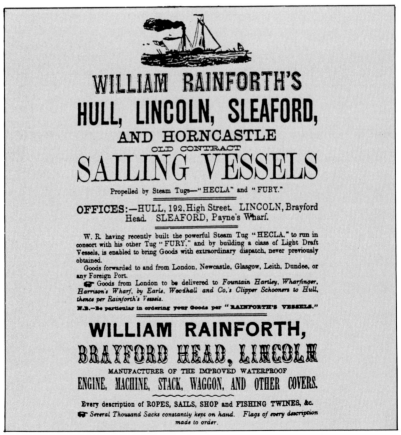

Advertisement by William Rainforth of Brayford Head, Lincoln relating to canal traffic to and from Horncastle c.1860.
From Local Studies Collection by courtesy of Lincolnshire Library Service

Chapter Four

Completion and Operation of the Canal

The canal, 11 miles in length with a fall of 84 ft was finally completed in 1802 for a total cost of £45,000, nearly four times the originally estimated figure. The locks along the canal going down from Horncastle were situated as follows (*see also Appendix Two*):

Horncastle (half mile south of)
Thornton (Lodge Hill)
Martin
Dalderby
Roughton
Haltham
Kirkby-on-Bain
Fulsby
Tumby
Coningsby
Tattershall
Tattershall (on Gibson Cut).

On Friday 17th September, 1802 a public holiday was called in Horncastle so that all people in the town could celebrate completion of the canal and its opening to traffic along its entire length from Horncastle to the River Witham.[21]

At one o'clock the vessels *Betsy* owned by J. Cuthill of Lincoln but registered in Horncastle, and *Martha* of Dalderby Wharf owned by Gilliatt & Wilson, Wharfingers of Church Lane, Horncastle, and the *British Queen* owned by Mr Boyers of Bridge Street Wharf, Horncastle entered the North and South Basins in turn, pulled slowly by ropes and dressed overall with flags and bunting. They were cheered by 2,000 spectators. A band situated on a pleasure boat owned by a Mr Lane played 'God Save the Queen', 'Rule Britannia', 'Hearts of Oak' and other rousing tunes. The shareholders of the canal company 'partook of a festive repast' at the Greyhound Inn then situated at the corner of East Street near the South Basin. The navvies and bankers who had worked on the canal celebrated on barges in both basins, and were supplied with free beer and food for the occasion. A few weeks afterwards the shareholders held a Ball to celebrate the opening:[22]

Horncastle Navigation. November 5 1802.
Notice is hereby given that this Navigation is now completed into the town of Horncastle, and open to all persons wishing to trade thereon.
N.B. Coals very much wanted.
The Company of Proprietors intend dining together at the Bull Hotel Horncastle Tuesday 9th November at 3 pm, where they will be happy to meet their Friends and all Well-wishers to the said Navigation.
N.B. There will be a Ball for the Ladies of the Town and Neighbourhood at the said Inn on Thursday the 11th instant. Dancing to begin at 7 pm.

In order to control the level of the water in the canal and South Ings Drain a sluice or staunch was erected at the confluence of the two rivers, and from

Horncastle Railway and Canal.

Reproduced from the 1904 25", Ordnance Survey M

Looking down the canal (Waring) from the South Basin. In the far distance the Waring can be seen turning left at the confluence with the Bain.

Confluence of the two rivers (the weir is a modern structure). The vessels turned left up the Bain for the North Basin or right for the South Basin of the canal.

there the canal had been extended into the town in two branch channels called the North and South Basins, each with its own wharf. The North Basin was on the River Bain to the south of the watermill, the South Basin being on the River Waring near the town bridge and onwards to near The Becks where the channel narrowed.

The original bed of the River Bain below the staunch was very twisting in its course, and in order to give better control of the water level thus improving drainage of the Great and Little Ings immediately south of the town, the Commissioners under the Horncastle Enclosure Award ordered that a new cut be made parallel to the canal, this new straight cut (often miscalled the Bain) to be called South Ings Drain. It eventually joined up with the Old Bain near Thornton. It was placed for ever under control of the Surveyor of Highways for Horncastle '. . . who as often as occasion shall be or require, shall cleanse out, scour, maintain, and keep the said drain'. The water flow was controlled in the drain by the staunch previously mentioned. The Dry Dock lay between it and the canal. The following entry in the *Stamford Mercury* refers:

> Horncastle Navigation.
> . . . It is necessary to hold a General Meeting of the said Proprietors for the purpose of taking into consideration the proposals of the Commissioners appointed for Inclosing and Improving the Open Lands within the said Parish of Horncastle, to cut and complete a drain of 12 ft bottom and 20 ft top, from the River Bain, in the front of Mr Heald's house, across the Waring branch of the said Navigation on to the southernmost point of the Little Ings below Thornton (Wind) Mill provided the Proprietors of the Navigation will erect a draw staunch or a pair of pointed doors in the South Bank of the said Navigation . . . Wm Bell; Wm Barton; Daniel Allenby; G. Lunn; T. Overton.

Thus it will be seen the South Ings Drain started from the loop which went towards the North Basin.

The works on the canal caused problems for millers and farmers, as already pointed out. In 1793 the millers at Fulsby and Kirkby-on-Bain watermills claimed damages for their mills being stopped through loss of water. Farmers also complained about losses due to flooding of their lands caused by canal works. The claims were agreed.

Trouble was never very far away, and in 1801 the Champion Lewis Dymoke of Scrivelsby Court objected to the line of the canal across his estate, accusing the Navigation Company of deviating from the original route. This was flatly denied by the company. The Champion's attendance at Committee Meetings ceased forthwith. In 1803 the company received notice from the Champion that he considered his rights in the waters of a stream running into the canal were valued at £600. He also claimed compensation over and above that already agreed for land covered by the embanking. In 1804 he claimed £400 for land excavated and covered by the canal banks, and £240 damages to a watermill. Further claims were made for dykes and culverts, for towpaths, and for seeping of water on to his lands, amounting in total to more than £1,000.[24] The company denied responsibility for most of the claims, but tried to negotiate a settlement without success. Meetings

The final stretch of the canal from the last lock before Horncastle. The water level would have been higher when the canal was working.

South Ings Drain looking south from Staunch. It joins the old bed of the River Bain further south.

were called, as the following notice in the *Stamford Mercury* indicates:[25]

> Horncastle Navigation.
> Whereas it appears to us, 5 of the Proprietors of the said Navigation whose names are hereunto subscribed, that it is necessary to hold a general meeting of the Proprietors for the purpose of taking into consideration the Demands made by the Hon. Lewis Dymoke on the said Navigation Company, for Lands covered by the Navigation Banks, the Injury done his Mill etc., etc.; and also to consider and determine upon whether any or what wharfage is to be taken for goods, wares and merchandise delivered at or upon the Company's wharfs — we do give notice that a Special General Meeting will be holden at the Bull Inn, Horncastle on Thursday 17th February at 10 am. Given under our hands the 17th January, 1803. J. Fretwell; Dan Allenby; Wm Walker; G. Lunn; Wm Barton.

The disagreements dragged on until 1810 when a case was filed at Lindsey Sessions where the Champion Lewis Dymoke claimed his lands, occupied by a Mr Adams, had been damaged,

> Due to leakage, oozing, and overflow of waters of the Navigation from the imperfect and improvident construction of the banks, and not providing culverts and other drains at proper places.

The judge ruled the Navigation Act in its clauses provided that in such a dispute Commissioners should be appointed to hear the complaints. As no such Commissioners had been appointed he ruled that his Court could not adjudicate on the action.[26]

The disputes were not resolved until the death of Lewis Dymoke in 1820 (the same year as the death of Sir Joseph Banks), when his successor the Reverend John Dymoke inherited the estate and title. He showed a more friendly attitude towards the canal company, and the previous claims were allowed to drop.

It is not clear why Lewis Dymoke changed his previous friendly attitude towards the canal company, when it will be remembered he leased land for a wharf at Dalderby at a peppercorn rent for 5 years. He was one of the original sponsors of the Parliamentary Bill, and one of the original shareholders, thus he was well disposed to the project in the first place. He was, however, a somewhat eccentric character, and given to bouts of heavy expenditure. The relevant entries in the Minutes Books, however, suggest the trouble originated from the decision to alter the route of the canal from Dalderby northwards, and make a new straight cut instead of following the course of the River Bain. The new cut crossed over much of the Champion's lands. His claim that the original line of the canal above Dalderby had been altered was true, and the Navigation Company was blatantly dishonest in denying it. Perhaps also there was a clash of personalities not revealed in documents. Lewis, who was a lifelong bachelor, succeeded to the Championship in 1784. His brother John, who was in holy orders, succeeded him in 1820. John's son Henry (later Sir Henry) succeeded him in 1828. He officiated as Champion at the coronation of George IV, and died in 1865.

In 1803 the 'Superintending Engineer' William Walker fell ill, and in 1804 George Douthwaite was appointed as superintendent of works to assist him

A section of Thornton Lock wall showing the Derbyshire dressed stonework, still in good condition.

Thornton Lock looking north. Note the guillotine gate fitted by the drainage authority. The old gate paddle mechanism appears to have been used for lowering and raising the gate. The railings are modern to safeguard grazing cattle from falling into the lock basin.

at a salary of £50 per annum with a rent free house. Shortly afterwards the committee asked Walker to resign as he was unfit for work on the canal, and Douthwaite took his place. He was a heavy drinker, however, and was reported to the committee 'for drinking in public houses instead of attending to the interest of the Company'. He died in 1810 leaving his widow destitute, and the committee instructed their Treasurer to allow her five guineas 'to enable her to travel back to her friends'.[27]

Supporting staff were then recruited in an effort to step up maintenance standards:[28,29,30]

Horncastle Navigation.
Wanted immediately, a sober, steady person, to superintend the Locks, Banks and Sluices of the said Navigation, and direct the necessary repairs thereof. All persons desirous of undertaking such trust are desired to deliver in their proposals to Mr Richard Clitherow of Horncastle, Treasurer to the Company on or before the 20th April next.

Horncastle Navigation.
General Annual Meeting Tuesday 30th September at 11 am. N.B. The Company being in want of a person to superintend the works of the said Navigation, and to keep the same in repair, will receive proposals in writing at their next meeting from any person who may think himself qualified to fill the situation.

Horncastle Navigation.
The Company are in want of a Carpenter, who has been accustomed to make lock and sluice doors: he will be expected to attend to the flood-gates and sluices in time of floods, and to keep the woodwork of the canal in repair. A liberal salary will be allowed.

In 1819 it was decided to appoint a Superintendent Maintenance Engineer and an assistant, and they were to inspect their respective lengths of the canal each day. The superintendent was based at Horncastle and his assistant at Kirkby-on-Bain, each being provided with a rent-free house:[31]

Horncastle Navigation.
To Superintendents of Navigations and Waterworks.
Wanted immediately, 2 steady middle-aged men, of good character, to superintend the Horncastle Navigation, in Lincolnshire. The Principal Superintendent must understand the letting of all sorts of navigation work by the rod floor and other-wise, and must also be acquainted with the building and repairing of locks, staunches, flood-gates, and bridges, and be able to let the same either to build or repair. The Principal Superintendent will have to walk 5 miles down the Navi-gation and back every day to examine the works, and to assist the traders up and down the river, as well as in time of flood to go down the whole line to examine the state of the works, and see that all staunches and flood gates are properly opened. There is a comfortable house and garden in the Town of Horncastle rent-free, and a salary of £50 a year will be given.
The second Superintendent will have to go down the navigation from the village of Kirkby to Tattershall, every day, a distance of six miles, and to assist the traders of the line as well as to attend to the floodgates and sluices in time of floods. A

Carpenter would be preferred, as he could be occasionally employed in making and repairing the locks and sluice doors. There is a good cottage and garden at Kirkby, rent-free, for the Second Superintendent, and a salary of £40 per annum will be allowed.

Rbt Clitherow, Clerk to the Company.

As already shown some of the earlier work on locks was of poor quality, and caused repairs to be carried out within a few years. Inadequate supervision over contractors was the main cause. Arthur Young visited Horncastle and inspected the canal — his comments were scathing:[32]

Horncastle Canal. Everything has been ill done for want of attention which Engineers ought to give — many thousands of pounds ill spent.

His comments give a clue as to why £25,000 had been spent well before the canal was finished, against an estimate of half that figure for the whole canal.

It has been suggested that the large size of bricks was one cause of the collapsed Tattershall Lock and of weirs, but the writer has discussed this with builders who suggest poor lime used in the mortar mix would be a more likely cause. This seems logical, because all the locks and weirs had to be repointed on a number of occasions. Also the use of poor lime in the mortar was referred to specifically by the committee as being one of the reasons for Cawley's dismissal. It was not large bricks which caused so many structural failures, but the original Engineer Cawley, who allowed contractors to use *mixed sizes* of bricks; thus stresses were not distributed evenly and distortions were caused under water pressure, resulting in collapse of walls. In June 1809 it was reported that all locks in the canal had to be repointed as water was seeping through the walls.

Another problem the company had to deal with was silting up of the canal bed, and it was decided to order a dredger, the following entry in the Minutes Books being relevant:

3rd January, 1810. Ordered that a Lighter be immediately built at the expense of the Company, of 20 tons burthen, and a machine for taking sand and gravel beds to be used in the lighter, and that it be built by Ben Gilliatt & William Walker.

The entry is interesting for two reasons. Firstly it is an example which shows boatbuilding took place in the town itself. Secondly Ben Gilliatt was a shareholder and member of the committee, and one cannot help wondering whether that had any influence of allotment of the contract. There does not appear to have been any request for tenders. However, that is pure conjecture.

The Town Criers of both Horncastle and Tattershall were used on occasions as well as advertisement in the *Stamford Mercury*:[33]

17.12.1811. A stone trough being sunk in the Navigation at Coningsby near Butts Bridge and an oak tree left floating in the same place — ordered our Clerk do advertise that if not claimed within a fortnight the same will be sold by auction, and that the same be cried in the market places of Horncastle and Tattershall.

In 1822 Samuel Bower the principal canal superintendent visited Derby-shire to assess various types of stone for lock repairs, and purchased an amount of stone from the Belper Stone Company. Some of the stone was to be cut and dressed before despatch. Part of the stone was used to repair the first lock:[34]

> Horncastle Navigation.
> Notice is hereby given that this Navigation will be stopped from the town of Horncastle to Dalderby Ford for 14 days from the 27th day of May to the 10th day of June next, for the purpose of taking down and re-building the first lock. By order of the Committee. Rt Clitherow, Clerk.

Vessels were not normally allowed to operate on Sundays, and the move-ment of boats during hours of darkness was not usually allowed, but in 1823 John Slack, proprietor of the Lincoln Packet pointed out to the committee that he had to wait at Lincoln for the boats from Hull until 10 or 11 am, on Fridays, and consequently could not reach Tattershall Lock until 6 or 7 o'clock in the evening, and as he was carrying goods as well as passengers it was essential in the interest of the traders in Horncastle that he should be able to meet the Carrier Carts from the villages in that town on Saturday, which was market day. The committee agreed that John Slack's Packet boat be allowed through the locks until 9 pm, on Fridays only.

In 1824 William Flower a toll collector appointed in 1821 bought a horse which he hired out to bargees for pulling their boats. Such enterprise was, however, stamped on firmly by the committee, and he had to sell the horse because as the committee stated '. . . it might form a connection between him and boatmen which might lead to bad consequences'.[35]

In 1839 the committee resolved that in view of frequent repair work on the canal, and necessary movement of wood, stone, bricks, tools, etc., it was necessary to purchase 'an old steam boat at an expense of £40 to be con-verted into a Lighter, and another boat has been thoroughly repaired, the necessary works requiring the almost constant use of two'. The legacy left by Cawley and the early contractors was still taking its toll!

Supervision of repair work was much improved after employment of the first two superintendents in 1819.

In the 1850s Richard Burnett was appointed Maintenance Engineer for the southern length of the canal, and lived at Kirkby-on-Bain. He is listed in White's Lincolnshire of 1856 rather grandly as Navigation Engineer.

Chapter Five
Collection of Tolls

There were four points along the canal where wharfage and toll charges were collected, the two main ones being at Lock No. 1 Tattershall, and Dalderby up to 1802. After completion of the canal in that year Horncastle was also a collection point.

The tolls allowed to be charged under the original Act of 1792 were as follows:

For goods passing along whole length of canal   2 shillings per ton
From River Witham to 7th lock   1s. 9d. per ton
From River Witham to 4th lock   1s. 3d. per ton

(Excepting lime, limestone, manure and road materials which were to be charged half the above tolls.)

Under the later Act of 1800 the tolls were increased considerably to:

For goods passing along whole length of canal   3s. 3d. per ton
From River Witham to 7th lock   2s. 7d. per ton
From River Witham to 4th lock   1s. 8d. per ton

(Excepting limestone, lime, manure and road materials which were to be charged half the above tolls.)

Extra tolls had to be paid on all vessels entering the River Witham, and in 1812 an Act (52 George III cap. 108) laid down byelaws regulating trade upon the Witham Navigation, and clauses were included relating to tolls on vessels from the Horncastle and Sleaford Canals entering the Witham (Loose Leaf Pamphlets L.C.R.L.):

> For all goods, wares, and merchandize liable to a toll or duty on the Horncastle and Sleaford Navigations or either of them, (if navigated or conveyed on any part of the River Witham) the present duty of nine Pence per ton, and a further toll or duty of one half of the amount now paid.
> For packet boats and other boats carrying passengers for hire, a toll or duty as and for two tons besides the tonnage, for the goods on board such packet or other boats.
> Skiffs and small vessels having less than one ton on board, and not carrying passengers for hire, and passing through any of the locks, to pay *one Shilling* beside the toll or duty for the goods on board such skiffs or vessels; but if two such skiffs or small vessels shall pass through the lock at the same time, then a toll or duty of *Sixpence* each shall be paid, besides the toll or duty for the goods on board.

At a specially convened general meeting held on the 18th April, 1850 the tolls were decreased (see schedule) in an effort to attract coal deliveries from the railway company, which shortly afterwards built a wharf and coal yard at Dogdyke where the coals were off loaded from trains and on to barges.

Cargo in the main consisted of coal, bricks, tiles, gravel and sand, iron, lime and fertilisers *up the canal*, and wool, wheat, oats, barley, gravel, malt and hides *down the canal*. General cargo for the town's shops and work-shops sometimes came by bargeload, and on occasions by boat direct from

NOTES.

That the Weights required to be used by the 5th and 6th. of William IV, cap. 63, viz.—

14lbs. to the Stone,

8 such Stones to the Hundred-weight, and

20 such Hundred-weights to the Ton,

shall be the Weight used on this Navigation.

All Goods, Wares, and Merchandise brought on this Navigation, to be considered Mixed Goods unless otherwise specifically named in the following Tables.

TABLE OF DUES,

~~PROPOSED~~ TO BE TAKEN ON THE

HORNCASTLE NAVIGATION.

[handwritten] as settled at a Special General Meeting of the Proprietors holden at the Bull Inn in Horncastle on the 18th day of April 1850 Confirmed at the annual General Meeting on the 17 October 1850

TABLE 3.

Articles conveyed.	Quantity.	Coningsby to Kirkby.	Coningsby to Horncastle.	Kirkby to Horncastle.
DUES UPWARDS FROM				
		s. d.	s. d.	s. d.
Coals,	per imp. ton	. 10	1 . 3	. 10
Lime,	,, ditto	. 10	1 . 5	. 10
Common Bricks,	400 to a ton	. 10	1 . 3	. 10
Floor Bricks,	500 ditto	. 10	1 . 3	. 10
Pan Tiles,	400 ditto	. 10	1 . 3	. 10
Oats, (not to exceed 24 st.)	per quar.	. 2	. 3	. 2
Barley (not to exceed 32 st.)	,, ditto	. 2¼	3 ½	. 2½
Wheat (not to exceed 36 st.)	,, ditto	. 3	. 4½	. 3
Malt,	,, ditto	. 2	. 3	. 2
Beans and Peas,	,, ditto	. 3	. 4¼	. 3
Fir Timber, per 50 feet to the imp. ton		1 . 3	2 . 0	1 . 3
Oak, Ash, and Elm, 40 feet to ditto		1 . 3	2 . 0	1 . 3
Deals, per 24, 12 ft. 3 by 11 to ditto		1 . 3	2 . 0	1 . 3
Wool, five sheets,	,, ditto	1 . 3	2 . 0	1 . 3
Stone, 15 feet,	,, ditto	1 . 3	2 . 0	1 . 3
Manure,	per imp. ton	. 9	1 . 0	1 . 0
Mixed Goods,	,, ditto	1 . 3	2 . 0	1 . 3

TABLE 4.

Articles conveyed.	Quantity.	to Coningsby.	to the Witham.
DUES DOWNWARDS from KIRKBY			
		s. d.	s. d.
Coals,	per imp. ton	. 10	1 . 3
Lime,	,, ditto	. 10	1 . 3
Common Bricks,	400 to a ton	. 10	1 . 3
Floor Bricks,	500 ditto	. 10	1 . 3
Pan Tiles,	400 ditto	. 10	1 . 3
Oats, (not to exceed 24 st.)	per quar.	. 2	. 3
Barley (not to exceed 32 st.)	,, ditto	. 2½	. 3¼
Wheat (not to exceed 36 st.)	,, ditto	. 3	. 11½
Malt,	,, ditto	. 2	. 3
Beans and Peas,	,, ditto	. 3	. 4¼
Fir Timber, per 50 feet to the imp. ton		1 . 3	2 . 0
Oak, Ash, and Elm, 40 feet to ditto		1 . 3	2 . 0
Deals, per 24, 12 ft. 3 by 11 to ditto		1 . 3	2 . 0
Wool, five sheets,	,, ditto	1 . 3	2 . 0
Stone, 15 feet,	,, ditto	1 . 3	2 . 0
Manure,	per imp. ton	. 9	1 . 0
Mixed Goods,	,, ditto	1 . 3	2 . 0

Tolls decided at a special meeting held on 18th April, 1850. The note at top right-hand corner reads, 'Pleasure Boats. At Annual Meeting 22nd October, 1851 it was resolved that Pleasure Boats be charged 1 shilling for passing 1 lock, 2 shillings for two locks and 3 shillings for 3 or more locks'.

TABLE 1.	TABLE 2.

DUES UPWARDS from the WITHAM.

Articles conveyed.	Quantity.	to Fulsby.	to Dalderby.	to Horncastle.
		s. d.	s. d.	s. d.
Coals,	per imp. ton	.10	1.3	1.8
Lime,	,, ditto			
Common Bricks,	400 to a ton	.10	1.3	1.8
Floor Bricks,	500 ditto			
Pan Tiles,	400 ditto			
Oats, (not to exceed 24 st.)	per quar.	. 2	. 3	. 4
Barley (not to exceed 32 st.)	,, ditto	. 2¼	. 3½	. 5
Wheat (not to exceed 36 st.)	,, ditto	.3	. 4¼	6
Malt,	,, ditto	. 2	. 3	. 4
Beans and Peas,	,, ditto	. 3	. 9½	. 6
Fir Timber, per 50 feet to the imp. ton		1.3	2.0	2.6
Oak, Ash, and Elm, 40 feet to ditto		1.3	2.0	2.6
's, per 24, 12 ft. 3 by 11 to ditto		1.3	2.0	2.6
Wool, five sheets,	,, ditto	1.3	2.0	2.6
Stone, 15 feet,	,, ditto	1.3	2.0	2.6
Manure,	per imp. ton	. 9	1.0	1.3
Mixed Goods,	,, ditto	1.3	2.0	2.6

DUES DOWNWARDS from HORNCASTLE.

Articles Conveyed.	Quantity.	to Kirkby.	to Coningsby.	to the Witham.
		s. d.	s. d.	s. d.
Coals	per imp. ton			
Lime	,, ditto			
Common Bricks,	400 to a ton	. 10	. 3	1.0
Floor Bricks,	500 ditto			
Pan Tiles,	400 ditto			
Oats, (not to exceed 24 st.)	per quar.	. 2	. 3	. 4
Barley (not to exceed 32 st.)	,, ditto	. 2½	. 3½	. 5
Wheat (not to exceed 36 st.)	,, ditto	. 3	. 4½	. 6
Malt,	,, ditto	. 2	. 3	. 4
Beans and Peas,	,, ditto	. 3	. 4½	. 6
Fir Timber, per 50 feet to the imp. ton		1.3	2 .	2.6
Oak, Ash, and Elm, 40 feet to ditto		1.3	2 .	2.6
Deals, per 24, 12 ft. 3 by 11 to ditto		1.3	2 .	2.6
Wool, five sheets	,, ditto	1.3	2 .	2.6
Stone, 15 feet,	,, ditto	1.3	2 .	2.6
Manure,	per imp. ton	. 9	1 .	1.3
Mixed Goods,	,, ditto	1.3	2 .	2.6

TABLE 5.

DUES DOWNWARDS from FULSBY.

Articles conveyed	Quantity.	to the Witham		
		s. d.	s. d.	s. d.
Coals,	per imp. ton	. 10		
Lime,	,, ditto	. 10		
Common Bricks,	400 to a ton	. 10		
Floor Bricks,	500 ditto	. 10		
Pan Tiles,	400 ditto	. 10		
Oats, (not to exceed 24 st.)	per quar.	. 2		
Barley (not to exceed 32 st.)	,, ditto	. 2½		
Wheat (not to exceed 36 st.)	,, ditto	. 3		
Malt,	,, ditto	. 2		
Beans and Peas,	,, ditto	. 3		
Fir Timber, per 50 feet to the imp. ton		1.3		
Oak, Ash, and Elm, 40 feet to ditto		1. 3		
Deals, per 24, 12 ft. 3 by 11 to ditto		1. 3		
Wool, five sheets,	,, ditto	1. 3		
Stone, 15 feet,	,, ditto	1. 3		
Manure,	per imp. ton	. 9		
Mixed Goods,	,, ditto	1. 3		

Dues on Gravel carried on any length of the Navigation sixpence per Ton

Mr Robert Nicholson
Collector of Downward Dues at Horncastle

Mr George Baker
Collector of upward Dues at Tattershall

Rich & Ro b Clitherow
Clerks

London. Some of the general merchants travelled to London each year to purchase goods direct from manufacturers or large wholesalers, then arranged for their transport by water direct to Horncastle. For instance in 1847 a trader vessel arrived in Horncastle from London carrying a full load of cargo for the shops (see advertisement page 26).

When the railway company was sponsoring its Bill for construction of a line from Kirkstead to Horncastle in 1854 part of its publicity included the statement 'The canal has never carried cattle', but see the Schedule of Tonnages (page 51) which includes sheep.

As will be seen from the toll sheets, tolls were levied on many types of goods at so much per ton or other weight. The main problem for the collectors of tolls was to check on the declared weights, and some boat captains cheated. However, the toll collectors soon became able to make a rough assessment by noting how deep the barge was settled in the water. No record has been found to suggest that the system of marking boats' hulls — weighing and gauging — in use on some canals was ever enforced on the Horncastle Navigation, although some boats arriving from other canals must have been so marked.

Most of the boats were owned by merchants, but a number were operated by 'Number Ones' — men who owned the vessel themselves and operated independently.

The collection of tolls and wharf fees would need men of some degree of education because written records had to be kept. It was, therefore, fortunate that the British and National Schools set up in the town in 1814 were soon educating the poorer sections of the population to a suitable standard to take on such work.[36]

Integrity was also important and bonds were insisted on. The first toll collector and lock keeper was appointed on 18th October, 1793 at a wage of 12 shillings per week. He was David North of Dogdyke, and he was taken on for duty at the lower Tattershall Lock. In that first month of October 1793 he collected £11 2s. 6d. in tolls. The committee gave an order for a lock house to be built for him, the dimensions to be 28½ ft long × 13½ ft wide. By 1795, however, the company was advertising for a replacement:[37]

Horncastle Navigation.
Wanted. A person to superintend the 1st Lock on the said Navigation, and to receive the tolls or dues payable thereat; to whom a reasonable salary will be allowed, and a comfortable dwelling house, rent-free. Any person inclined to offer himself is requested immediately to deliver his proposals to Mr Rd Clitherow, Attorney, in Horncastle. N.B. Sufficient security will be expected for the faithful discharge of the office.

A similar advertisement in 1820 required a surety of £300:[38]

Horncastle Navigation.
Wanted. A steady man who can be recommended for honesty and integrity, to receive the Tolls at Tattershall Lock. A liberal salary will be allowed with a comfortable house rent and tax free. The testimonials and recommendations to be sent within 21 days from the date hereof to the office of Mr Clitherow, Attorney, Horncastle. A Bond with a sufficient surety to the amount of £300 for the due performance of the office will be expected.

A List of the Quantity of Sundry Goods estimated at a Ton on the
Horncastle Navigation

Coals 1 chaldron	Potatoes 13 Pecks	Co 13 & 19½ … Deals	Osier Groundsels
Pitts Malt wort	Uns.d Staves or 40 feet	Plunder Battins	Stone Slacks
Cork 10 Quarters Barley … 6 do	Fir Timber 50 do	Flats … 500	Hay 20 Hundred
Wheat Meal or Flour	Bricks or Pantile 500	Laths … 250	Glass 7 Crates
Rape and … meal	Flax … 1000	Grocery and Dry Whs …	Hemp, feet 40
Seeds 5 Quarters	Oil Cake 6 … or ……	Flour 1 Wt …	Cork … 100
White Lime 1⅔ do	Hops … 2 Pipes	Wool & Gratis … Packs	Stone 16 Cwt
Slacked Lime 2 do	Oil Cloth … 120	Gen Average &c … 250	Flagstone 10 … cu. yds.
Lime Stone A ton	Flat Botts 60 … …	Smells & … 300	
	Pipes & Tyles 90 & 120	Fish … 20	

In fact the salary offered was £60 per annum. Such a salary when a bond of £300 was required may seem low, but it was twice the agricultural wage at that time, and the work was far from arduous.

Not a lot is known about the toll collectors, but some certainly fell short of the required standards:

John Crow	Appointed in 1819 — dismissed shortly afterwards for allowing overweight vessels through the locks.
Ben Sharpe	Dismissed for frequent drunkenness.
William Flower	He was toll collector from 1821 to 1848. He had his salary of £60 per annum raised to 70 in 1838 — a sign of the canal's growing prosperity and presumably in appreciation of his long and faithful service.

In the 1850s other toll keepers were:

Robert Nicholson	At Horncastle wharf.
Richard Harrison	At Horncastle wharf, 1856.
Clitherow Smith	Tattershall, 1856.
George Baker	Tattershall. He was still collecting tolls in 1883.
C. Gould	Collected the last tolls in the 1880s.

Staunch Cottage Horncastle. The cottage was erected to house the Staunchkeeper. He had to be readily available particularly in times of flood or drought, when timely operation of the staunch gates was vital to the operation of the canal.

The toll collectors also had to supervise operation of the locks, and report to the Secretary any breaking of rules so that consideration could be given to prosecution. Entries in Horncastle Petty Sessions Minutes given below are typical of many:

27.3.1830   Henry Love Boatman convicted of wantonly drawing the slacker of the fourth lock belonging to Horncastle Navigation and thereby wasting the water to the prejudice of the said Navigation on the 27th March 1830 at the Parish of Dalderby and was fined £2 penalty and nine shillings cost.

4.4.1832   William Spicer of Horncastle, master of a vessel called Lincoln Trader — fined £5 for giving a false account of his lading.

13.7.1850   William Taylor — convicted of giving a false account of his boat's lading to the Collector of Tolls on the Horncastle Navigation. Fined £5 and ordered to pay the additional toll of 5 shillings and one pence.

27.7.1878   Mowbray Faunt, Boatman, convicted of drawing slacker of Fulsby Lock to prejudice of Fulsby Mill. Fined £2.

Mowbray Faunt was mainly occupied in taking gravel from Kirkby-on-Bain to Tattershall and Boston, but in 1883 he took a load of 20 tons of wheat from Horncastle to Lincoln (*see following toll sheets*). Other prosecutions were taken out against farmers for washing sheep in the canal, for throwing debris therein, and against other people for swimming in the locks.

White's Lincolnshire 1856 lists Leonard Wilkinson and James Fox of Horncastle as Wharf Clerks, showing the establishment of the canal had created white-collar jobs as well as manual employment in the town. Thomas May was listed as Steam Packet Agent.

Landowners with lands or houses adjoining the canal were permitted under the Horncastle Navigation Acts to use pleasure craft and other small boats on the canal without payment, except for dues when passing through the locks. They were then charged at the same rate as a barge carrying three tons of cargo.

View of Brayford showing general duty barge and sailing keel. Rainforth's warehouse and wharf can be seen on left of the picture. Vessels to and from Horncastle passed through the swing bridge seen in centre of picture. The bridge tollkeeper's hut is shown adjacent to the bridge.

From Local Studies Collection by courtesy of Lincolnshire Library Service

Various Boats –

Horncastle Navigation.	Dues collected by *George Baker*			for the Month of *Aug & Sep*				
Date 1883	Captain's Name.	Taken on Board.	Delivered.	Description.	Tons.	Cwt.	Per Ton.	£
Aug 2	W Upsall	Hirbey	Boston	Gravel	26	6	–	–
2	R Saum	Do	Witham	Do	10	6		
2	J Skinner	Do	Bos.	Do	22	6		
Sep 14	Garfitt Esq	Shooting Party		—	1		/6	
25	W Lathorp	Ups.	Con &	Coal	39		/6	1.0
26	W Upsall	Kir	Bos.	Gravel	26		6	1
27	Garfitt Esq	Shooting Party		—	1		/6	
	Total for August & Sep months			—	—	—		4.3

		£ s d		
1883	July month –	22. 17 – 0		
	August & September	4. 3. 0	*Scarcity of water*	
Total to End Sep 36th =		27 – 0. 0	*Witham*	
	1883			

NB J Skinners & J Upsalls Cargoes were
July Carried forward to October month
& in Collectors Hands for Change –

Signed
George Baker
Collector

Toll sheets for 1883. Note comment re. shortage of water in River Witham. The shooting party was organised by Mr Garfitt of Garfitt & Claypons Bank, no doubt entertaining customers.

Various Boats

Horncastle Navigation.   Dues collected by Geo Baker   for the Month of November 18 83

Captain's Name.	Taken on Board.	Delivered.	Description.	Tons.	Cwt.	Per Ton.	£	Amount s	d
Jos Upsall	Nav^n =	Boston	Sand	32		6		16	-
Jos Upsall	Do	Do	Sand	24		6		12	
W Upsall	Do	Do	Sand	25		6		12	6
"	Con Gass House	Do	Gasswater	2		1/0		2	-
Jos Upsall	Kir	Do	Gravel	24		6		12	
R Faunt	Hlstle	Lincoln	110 wheat	22		1/0	1	2	-
R Faunt	Kir	Bos	Gravel	24		6		12	-
Jos Upsall	Do	Do	Do	24		6		12	-
W Upsall	Nav	Do	Sand	23		6		12	6
Jos Upsall	off Bank	Do	Sand	20		6		10	-
T Skinner	Kir	Do	Gravel	22		6		11	-
Jos Upsall	Do	Do	Do	24		6		12	-
R Faunt	Do	A Gows	Do	24		6		12	-
R Faunt	Do	Bos	Do	24		6		12	-
Jos Upsall	Nav	Do	Sand	24		6		12	-
T Skinner	Kir	Do	Gravel	22		6		11	-
T Scarboro	YRs up	Con &c	Coal	50		1/0	2	10	-
Do	Con &c Down	Lincoln	110 wood	27	15	1/0	1	7	9
Jos Upsall	Kir	Bos	Gravel	24		6		12	-
T Skinner	Do	Do	Do	22		6		11	-
T Wright	Small Boat for Willows			1		1/0		1	-
1883 Total November Month							£	14 14	9

Toll sheet of 1883. Note wheat was still being sent down whole length of canal, then on to Lincoln via River Witham.

Horncastle Navigation.	Dues collected by *C Gould*		for the Month of *October* 18					
ate.	Captain's Name.	Taken on Board.	Delivered.	Description.	Tons.	Cwt.	Per Ton.	Amo
3	E Gilbert	Horncastle	Lincoln	Wheat	30	0	1/-	1 10
5	R Jaunt	Kirkby	Boston	Gravel	24	0	6	12
12	J Upsall	Coningsby	''	''	24	0	6	12
13	W Upsall	''	''	''	26	0	6	13
15	W Laythorpe	Tumby	Lincoln	Wood	12	0	1/-	12
20	W Upsall	Coningsby	Boston	Gravel	26	0	6	13
23	W Laythorpe	Dogdyke	Coningsby	Coal	17	0	1/-	17
30	J Upsall	Coningsby	Boston	Sand	24	0	6	12
								£6 1
85		*November Month*						
12	J Scarboro		Coningsby	Coal	45	0	1/-	2 5
13	W Laythorpe		''	''	38	0	1/-	1 18
								£4 3
85		*December Month*						
7	J Upsall	Coningsby	Boston	Gravel	24	0	6	12
7	E Gilbert	Horncastle	Lincoln	Barley	34	0	6	17
17	J Upsall	Coningsby	Boston	Gravel	24	0	6	12
21	do	''	''	''	24	0	6	12
21	E Gilbert	Horncastle	Lincoln	Barley	24	0	6	12
22	do	''	''	''	18	0	6	9
24	J Upsall	Coningsby	Boston	Sand	24	0	6	12
								£4 6

Toll sheet 1885. Note corn still being sent down whole length of canal to Lincoln.

To all Persons *navigating* on the *River Witham*, or the Cuts and Trenches thereof.

WE the Leffees of the faid River, Cuts, and Trenches, deem it neceffary to give this public Notice, (accompanied by an Abftract from the Act of Parliament ordered to be printed by the Commiffioners of the Navigation of the faid River,) for the better Information not only of the Navigators paffing up and down the fame, but to all others having Intereft or Concern in the Conveyance thereby of any Goods, Wares, Merchandizes, and Commodities whatfoever, — THAT we ourfelves and alfo on our Behalf, *William Stephenson* at *Bofton Lock*, *Thomas Pilley* at *Kirkftead Lock*, and *Joseph Crow* at *Lincoln Lock*, are legally appointed Collectors, and are empowered to receive the Tolls arifing upon the faid River, Cuts, and Trenches. And we alfo for the greater Accommodation of the Public, have appointed *Daniel North*, Lock-Keeper at the *firft Lock* upon the *Horncaftle Navigation* neareft to the faid *River Witham*; And alfo *Hugh Mountain Fox*, Lock-Keeper at the *firft Lock* upon the *Sleaford Navigation* neareft to the faid *River Witham*, to be Collectors and Receivers of fuch of the Tolls becoming due unto us upon all Goods, Wares, Merchandizes, and Commodities whatfoever that fhall be carried or conveyed up or down that Part of the faid River running and lying between the *two Locks* thereon, called or known by the Names of *Bofton Lock* and *Kirkftead Lock*, and that do not pafs through the fame or either of them.

Jos. Morris.
Mich. Pilley.

LINCOLN, November 12, 1794.

It is interesting that there appears to have been co-operation between the Lessees of the navigation rights on the River Witham, and the Horncastle Navigation Company and Sleaford Navigation Company over the collection of tolls on the Witham itself. It appears to have been agreed between them that the Lock-keepers at the lower locks on the two canals should not only collect tolls from vessels travelling up the canals, but also from vessels using that stretch of the Witham between the entrances to the two canals.   *L.C.R.L. Loose Pamphlets L.386 UP. 2130*

Quality.	Quantity.	Weight.	Quality.	Quantity.	Weight.
		Tons. Cwt.			Tons. Cwt.
Coals - - - -	One Chaldron	1 .3 ·	Five feet and half		
Coak - - - -	100 Strike -	1 —	Pofts	90 - . - -	1 —
Oats Malt or Bark	10. Quarters	1 —	Single Deals - -	Half hundred -	1 —
Barley and Rape	7 Quarters	1 —	Double Deals -	Quarter hund⁴.	1 —
Wheat, Beans,			Battens - - -	1 hundred · -	1 —
and Peas	5 Quarters	1 —	Thatch Reed -	5 hundred	
Whole Lime - -	1 Chal. and ¼ -	1 —		Bunches	1 —
Slecked Lime -	2 Chaldrons -	1 —	Grocerys - - -	2 Hogfheads -	1 —
Potatoes - - -	130 Pecks - -	1 —	Woad - - - -	1 D⁰ - - -	¼ —
Timber, Oak,			Spetches - - -	8 Packs . - -	1 —
Afh, or Elm	40 Feet. - -	1 —	Squares at 9 inches	250 - - - -	1 —
Fir Timber - -	50 Feet - -	1 —	Sheep - - - -	20 - . - -	1 —
Bricks - - -	5 hundred ⸴ -	1 —	Porter - - - -	6 Barrels - -	1 —
Flat Tiles - -	One thoufand	1 —	Flour - - - -	8 Sacks - -	1 —
Pan Tiles - -	500 - - -	1 —	Seeds - - - -	10 Quarters -	1 —
Oil Cakes - -	6 Ponnds and⎫		Glass - - - -	12 whole Crates	1 —
	a half a Pair ⎬ 1 —		Hemp Seed - -	40 Strike - -	1 —
	one thoufand ⎭		Polts 4½ feet - -	120 - - - -	1 —
Other Oil Cakes			Pavement Bricks	300 - - . -	1 —
in Proportion	. . .		Stone - - - -	16 Cubic Feet -	1 —
Wine - - - -	2 Pipes - -	1 —	Paving Stone -	10 Superf¹ y⁴ˢ	1 —
Felloes - - - -	120 - - - -	1 —	Pots - - - -	6 Crates - -	1 —
Seven feet Pofts -	60 - . - -	1 —			

All other Goods, Wares, Merchandize, and Commodities, not mentioned in the above Schedule, to be eftimated and paid for after the Rate of Two thoufand Two hundred and Forty Pounds *per* Ton.

Schedule of ton equivalents for River Witham. The Witham Navigation Act 1808 included a schedule of ton equivalents to help toll-keepers dealing with vessels travelling on the River Witham itself. The charges are almost the same as those laid down by the Horncastle Navigation Company for the canal. *L.C.R.L. Loose Pamphlets*

REPORT.

To the Company of Proprietors of the Horncastle Navigation, in the County of Lincoln.

Gentlemen,

Your Commitee have the pleasure of reporting an increase of traffic during the past year, and a consequent slight increase in dues as compared with the previous year, and this notwithstanding the continued and (as it appears to your Committe) the somewhat vexatious stoppage of the River Witham at the Bardney Lock.

The reduction of the working staff effected last year, has been the means of keeping down the working expenses which are now reduced to a minimum.

The silting up of the North Basin of the Navigation has caused a considerable outlay in clearing it, but notwithstanding this heavy item in the Treasurer's accounts, your Committee recommend a Dividend of £1 10s. 0d. per cent.

Dated 24th October, 1871.

GEO. GILLIAT,
DAVID CUSSONS,
A. C. R. ADCOCK,
ROBt. C. ARMSTRONG,
JOHN H. W. SCOTT,
ROBt. CLITHEROW.

Chapter Six

The Effects of the Canal on the Town of Horncastle and District

It is an undeniable fact that the opening of the Horncastle Navigation not only brought prosperity to the town, but altered its character from what was really a large inland village to that of a thriving market town and centre of local government.

The population of Horncastle more than doubled between 1801 and 1851, from 2,015 to 4,921, but the canal was one factor only amongst others responsible for that. The natural increase of births over deaths was one of the main causes of the explosion of population, and enclosure of the open fields in 1805 resulted in release of land for building houses. However, the canal opened up opportunities for the establishment of new businesses, and the expansion of existing ones.

For instance James Grounsell had a workshop down Spilsby Road where he made early threshing machines. A brass foundry powered by a watermill was opened on the banks of The Thunker, and Hopton Iron Works on The Wong was opened by William Ashton who made farm implements, specialising in harrows which were sold all over Great Britain.

In 1792 there was one wool merchant only, C. Richardson, and he combined trade with farming. By 1826 two more wool merchants had started business, one of them, Henry Turner, building a warehouse on the south basin. Before the opening of the canal farmers had their fleeces wound by itinerant woolwinders, and dealt direct with travelling wool factors from Yorkshire and the Midlands who had a bad reputation for swindling the farmers. An item in the *Stamford Mercury* in 1788 referred to that fact: 'We have sworn brokers, appraisers and auctioneers — why should the wool factor be exempt — the poor laborious woolwinder is either bound by oath or otherwise subject to heavy and severe penalties should he be guilty of fraud, . . .'

A well known Lincolnshire woolwinder who gained national fame in the Methodist Church as a preacher was Charles (Thrasher) Richardson of Tetford near Horncastle.

In 1792 there were no coal merchants, or corn merchants, but by 1826 there were nine in business, five of them with premises on the waterside. Large quantities of corn and wool went down the canal; for instance in 1825 30,000 quarters of corn and 3,000 sheets of wool were despatched to Boston and Lincoln.[39] Much of the wool went to Yorkshire mills. Coal was brought from the Midland collieries in large quantities, and the price in the town was halved. A steady supply of coal in large quantities was needed by the Horncastle Gas Light and Coke Co., which started business in 1833, thus the canal was indirectly involved in lighting the town by gas when the Lighting and Watching Act was adopted in the town.

Kelly's Directory of 1855 lists the firm of Hill & Kirk barge owners of Horncastle and conveying coal from Yorkshire and Derbyshire. In 1847 and into the 1850s, William Dixon corn and coal merchant of East Street, Horn-

Carrier carts beside the south basin of the canal on market day. Note the warehouse of the Phoenix Brewery, one of many large warehouses erected on the south basin. People came in by carrier cart from surrounding villages to catch steam packets to Lincoln and Boston.

Horncastle High Street on market day c.1880.

Cussons' Compendium of Local Information.

CARRIERS' CARTS WHICH REGULARLY ATTEND HORNCASTLE MARKET.

Towns and Villages	Carrier's Name		Inn in Horncastle
Alford	Blow		George
Ditto	Reed		Red Lion
Barkwith	Winter	Overton	Ditto
Belchford	Sutton	Dawson	Rodney
Ditto	Hudson		Ditto
Bag Enderby	Bark		Greyhound
Bardney	Simpson		Maids' Heads
Benniworth	Kent		George
Ditto	Tacey		Fighting Cocks
Bucknall	Thlson		Ditto
Baumber	Brackenbury		Black Horse
Coningsby	Cooling		Maid's Heads
Goulceby	Tomlinson		Ditto
Ditto	Hatcliffe		Rodney
Hamringham	Rouse		White Hart
Hemingby	Cade		New Inn
Ditto	Langley		Rodney
East Kirkby	Martin		George
Fulletby	Pickett		Rodney
Kirkstead	Sharpe	Brookes	White Hart
Langton by Wragby	Melbourne		Ditto
Louth	Cash		Maids' Heads
Ditto	Badley		Rodney
Ditto	Swaby		Maids' Heads
Ditto	Broadbent		Red Lion
Mareham-le-Fen	Codd		Maids' Heads
Ditto	Chapman		George
Martin Fen	Cawdon		Fighting Cocks
Minting	Carturght		Black Horse
Ditto and Gautby	Day		White Hart
New Bolingbroke	Newham		George
Ditto	Wood		Maids' Heads
Old Bolingbroke	Wilson		Ditto
Ditto	Scrimshaw		George
Sleaford	Edwards		Ditto
Scamblesby	Crowson		Red Lion
Spilsby	Wydle		George
Ditto	Green		Ditto
Stixwold	Warrington		White Hart
Tetford	Brackenbury		Ship
Ditto	Carter		Greyhound
Tattershall Thorpe	Kent		Maids' Heads
Tattershall	Fowler		Ship
Wragby and Lincoln	Brown		Maids' Heads
Ditto	Weldon		Black Horse
Tumby	Furniss		Queen's Head

This list of Carrier Carts from the *Horncastle Compendium* of 1845 shows how important the town had become as a market centre to the surrounding villages. The carts converged on the town on market days and Fairs from all points of the compass, loaded with country produce and villagers. It is an ironic fact that the villages listed do not now have public transport of any kind.

castle was acting as agent for Harrison's Wharf of St Katherine's Dock, London handling goods for shops direct from London.

Iron for tools and agricultural implements, urgently needed due to improved methods of farming, came from Staffordshire and Yorkshire. Linseed oil cake and guano came from Hull, and by 1826 there were four druggists acting as agents for its distribution in the villages. Also by 1826 four timber merchants and three maltsters had started in business.[40]

By 1856 there were 7 artificial manure dealers, 12 coal and corn merchants, and 5 woolstaplers. Bankers were quick to see their opportunity, and by 1819 Garfit, Claypons & Co., were established on the waterside, and Lincoln and Lindsey Banking Company in the Corn Market (now Bull Ring) in 1833. A Savings Bank had also been established in 1817. A Marine Store dealer Mr John Burrell had a shop in North Street, and Thomas Haddock kept a boat chandlers shop in St Lawrence Street near the North Basin of the canal. In 1836 a poll for a special church rate was taken in Horncastle, and thirteen boatmen were listed as residing in the town. Also Thomas Wilkinson was listed as Boatwright.

The loop to the North Basin and the basin area itself were the most heavily industrialised areas of the town. On the loop wharfs were tanneries, fellmongers and bone dealers' yards, coal yards, boat builders' yards, wool and corn warehouses, carpenters' workshops, artificial manure, salt and lime merchants' sheds, and fishmongers.

Adjacent to the wharfs of the North Basin itself were malt kilns and two windmills. The area down Saint Lawrence Street or Pudding Lane at the rear of the Post Office (now a car park) was closely packed with industries and trades. A tannery and curriers workshop owned by Briggs & Shera was the largest employer of labour in the town. As well as the tannery and curriers business, Briggs & Shera had their own boot and shoe factory. John Panton had his wholesale boot and shoe factory, and Charles Caborn, saddler, had his workshop conveniently nearby.

On the St Lawrence Street site there were also basket makers, coal merchants, cutlers, gasfitters, ironmongers, steel merchant, marine store dealer for boats, nail maker, tinner and brazier, blacksmith, saddler, currier, dyer, coachbuilder, furniture broker, tobacco pipe manufacturer, glover, and plumber.

Bill of lading – coal from Yorkshire.

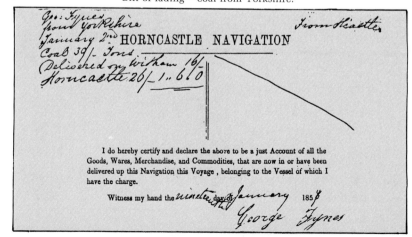

Approaching the last lock before Horncastle.

Remains of the last lock before Horncastle (railings modern). Note excellent condition of stonework.

Wool dealer's warehouse and wharf in Bridge Street at the centre of the town. The warehouse was built as late as 1865 on the loop leading to the north basin. Woolpacks were loaded on to the vessels down the winch chute shown at the end of the building. Other warehouses can be seen at the side of the canal to the left of the photograph. At the time of the photograph, c.1920, the warehouse and road were under repair.

This huge warehouse was completed in 1802 just before the canal reached Horncastle, and was used mainly for corn wharfage. The builders used part of the Roman wall of the town for its foundations, which can be seen in the County library building erected on the site when the warehouse was demolished. A coal merchant's yard where coal was delivered by barge was situated behind the wall. The warehouse was on the south basin.

Change and Growth of Trade & Industry from 1792 to 1836 as shown by Numbers of Workers

	1792	1836
Brick & Tile Makers	1	3
Bricklayer	4	27
Clog Maker	2	1
Coal & Corn Dealer	1	9
Carpenters & Joiners	2	25
Chairmakers	2	3
Coopers	2	5
Farmers	15	14
Glover & Breeches Maker	3	–
Braziers & Tinplate Worker	1	5
Ironmonger & Pattern Maker	1	3
Inn & Beerhouse Keepers	19	29
Leather Cutter & Currier	1	3
Linseed Cake Merchant	–	6
Millwright & Machine Maker	–	2
Maltsters	4	5
Miller	3	4
Peruke Maker	4	–
Plumber & Glazier	4	5
Saddler	2	4
Spinningwheel Maker	1	–
Shoemakers	11	51
Rope Maker	–	6
Tanners & Fellmongers	3	7
Tea Dealer	1	2
Timber Merchants	–	5
Watch & Clockmakers	3	4
Weaver	1	–
Wooldealer	1	3
Woolcomber*	1	1
Wheelwright	1	5
Coachbuilder & Harness Maker	–	1
Blacksmith & Farrier	6	19
Brewers	–	7
Boatmen	–	15
Boatwright	–	1
Druggist	–	5
Sawyer	–	6
Merchants	–	9
Labourers, General	–	145

* Increased to 5 by 1856.

The above details have been taken from *Universal British Directory of Trade Commerce & Manufacture* Volume 3 pages 285–289. London 1792; and *Account of Persons Assessed to the Poor Rate, Horncastle, 1836* (L.C.R.L. Pamphlets). Similar information is available in the various editions of *White's Lincolnshire* from 1826 onwards, but usually only master craftsmen or master tradesmen are listed, whereas the above 1836 source gives numbers of journeymen also, thus a better picture of the numbers of people working in the various trades and crafts is obtained. Professions, Gentry, Clergy and services such as shopkeepers have not been included. Most of the farmers listed in 1836 were in the town's Wildmore Fen Allotments.

Dealing in the building, sale and repair of boats was carried on in the town. Benjamin Gilliatt and William Walker had a boat building yard at the bottom of Church Lane, and Thomas Wilkinson a boat building business and wharf near Bow Bridge in Bridge Street. We have already seen that Gilliatt and Walker built a lighter and dredger for the Canal Company, of 20 tons burthen. They were advertising for business in the *Stamford Mercury* in 1816:

> 26.1.1816   HORNCASTLE. To Watermen and others. To be sold by Private Contract. An excellent clinker-built sloop with mast, sails, rigging and every other necessary requisite for the Yorkshire trade. Price and particulars may be known by applying to Mr B. Gillerr [sic] Horncastle.

> 23.2.1816   HORNCASTLE. James B. Cuttill having established boats and commenced the carrying trade between Lincoln and Horncastle, solicits the support of his friends and public.

Cuthill had already been operating a ketch from Dalderby as early as 1801, and a sloop between Horncastle and Wakefield in 1807.

A number of local carpenters and joiners applied their craft skills to boat building. For instance in 1792 the firm of Boyers and Harrison were in business as brickmakers, builders, upholsterers, joiners and carpenters. A few years later Daniel Boyers was building boats on the canal side in Bridge Street, and erected a workshop and store there which is still standing with his name carved on a stone plaque. Walker and Wilkinson previously mentioned were both carpenters by trade.

The Directors of the canal company had their own boat built by Thomas Wilkinson. It was later fitted with glass sides and doors, and the Directors went on annual outings and voyages of inspection down the whole length of the canal. It was the custom on such inspection trips for the committee to have a meal in the house of the toll collector at Tattershall Lock. A note by the collector in 1868 shows they did not stint themselves for food, which was given by members. The collector, Smith, stated that after the meal the remainder of the food was given to him and his wife. It included a roast of chine of beef, lean part of a hare, parts of two fowls, one pound of cheese, three loaves of bread, and a quantity of ale and porter. Mrs Smith was given a gratuity of 8s. 6d. for preparing the lunch and waiting at table. Potatoes for the meal were supplied by Smith from his garden.[41]

As well as vessels carrying goods, steam packets were used to carry passengers. The packet boats started in service on the River Witham in 1814, and by 1817 they were providing regular services between Lincoln and Boston, but the early packet owners did not operate up the canals. People in Horncastle wishing to travel to Lincoln or Boston by water had to make a long road journey to Kirkstead Wharf and catch the packets there, as the following note from the *Horncastle Compendium* relates:

> Riggall's two horse van leaves the Maids' Heads Inn every morning (except Sundays) at eight and one for Woodhall Baths and Kirkstead, where it meets the Steam Packet for Lincoln and Boston. A Sociable also leaves the above Inn on Wednesday mornings at five o'clock to meet the Lincoln Packet at Kirkstead for Boston Market, and returns to Horncastle after the arrival of the Boston Packet at Kirkstead in the evening; and on Friday mornings at five o'clock to meet the Boston Packet for Lincoln Market and returns in the evening.

However, a regular passenger service by packets from Horncastle was soon established, and by 1826 the following vessels were listed in *White's Lincolnshire* as running:

> *Horncastle–Boston.* The James and Mary Packet from Waterside on Tuesday mornings. Goods & passengers.
> *Horncastle–Lincoln.* A Regular Trader carrying goods and passengers from Mr. Gilliatt's Wharf, Church Lane.
> *Horncastle–Nottingham, Manchester, Wakefield, Leeds.* Regular Trader from West Street Wharf by Thomas Armstrong.

In 1842 the following vessels were running:

> *Horncastle–Boston.* Read's Packet leaves South Basin Horncastle on Tuesday mornings for Boston at 7 am, where it arrives in the evening; leaves Boston on Friday mornings at 7 am and arrives in Horncastle in the evening.
> *Horncastle–Lincoln.* Slack's Packet leaves Horncastle on Tuesday mornings at 7 am, for Lincoln where it arrives in the evening. Returns Horncastle Saturdays.
> *To Hull, Selby & Leeds.* Regular Traders from George Gilliatt's Wharf bottom of Church Lane.

Packets continued to be viable financially long after the railway had started to operate, for instance:

> In 1862 *Horncastle–Lincoln.* Thorpe's Packet leaves Horncastle for Lincoln every Tuesday morning and returns on Saturdays.
> In 1872 *Horncastle–Boston & Lincoln.* Regular Trader boat each week from Alfred Healey's Wharf near Manor House. (Healey was also a maltster, brewer and spirit merchant.)

Owners of the passenger packets at the start of the services had to pay a toll of 2s. for the voyage down the canal, but if the packet went on from there on the River Witham the Witham Company charged a toll of 6s. In 1817 the committee of Horncastle Navigation Company had decided that Captains of Packets would have to pay a toll of 3d. per passenger, but soon reverted to an overall toll for the boat along the length of the canal.

The appearance and character of the town was altered in many ways. Although stage coaches and heavy goods wagons which had made the inns the social and business centres were still operating in the first half of the nineteenth century, the focus quickly moved to the waterside. Wharfs were built on the north and south basins, and large warehouses of three or four storeys with up to eight bays were erected. A large Corn Exchange was built in the High Street in 1856. Barges were the centre of a bustling activity, loading and unloading their goods on and off carts and wagons, and passenger packets embarked or disembarked their passengers for and from Lincoln and Boston. Wharfingers, tradesmen, agents, clerks, toll collectors, customs men and checkers were always busy about the scene. Many new jobs were created, and goods on sale in the shops increased in variety. Coal became plentiful and cheap, and people no longer had to endure perishing cold throughout the winter. Not all effects of the canal, however, were beneficial to the town.

The explosion of population already mentioned resulted in the establishment of numerous beer shops, public houses, and brothels, some of which were on or near the waterfronts. It is not surprising, therefore, that boatmen and navvies or bankers were in trouble at times with the watchmen and constables. For instance in 1844 the town constables reported to the Commissioners of Lighting and Watching as follows:[42]

> A new beerhouse of the lowest type has been opened in Saint Lawrence Lane just off Dog Kennel Yard near the north basin of the canal. Daft the landlord runs it not only as a drink place, but also as a lodging house and brothel, especially for vagrants, boatmen and canal bankers.
>
> A party in the King's Head of the worst characters in town. Went in. They scattered. Brown went over the bridge by the waterside. Ingoldby and another went up Union Street. The whole party met again in the Wong. Sharpe and Brown were together for a good bit after in a boat belonging to William Coppins.

A year later canal bankers were still causing trouble:

> April 1845. Sunday morning about 11 o'clock there was a party of tramps and lodging house people turned out of Daft's, drunk who went into the churchyard and insulted Mr Geo. Gilliatt and family on their way to church . . . Same evening just about 6 o'clock another party of canal bankers turned out of Daft's tap drunk. One of the men began to make water just against Mrs Clayton's window.

The large quantities of goods in the canal warehouses attracted the attention of thieves, many incidents being reported in the *Stamford Mercury*, and the reports give some idea of the goods stored by the Wharfingers. In November 1842, 200 fleeces of wool were stolen from a warehouse situated on the waterside near where the Library now stands. Mr Fox of Scrivelsby who rented the warehouse offered a reward of £50 for apprehension of the thief. In view of the bulky nature of the fleeces they must have been smuggled on to a barge and out of the town down the canal.

In 1844 tobacco was the temptation. Sixty pounds of tobacco were stolen from a cask in a warehouse belonging to a Mr Glazier. In 1845, 70 pounds of shag tobacco were stolen from a warehouse occupied by Mr J. Calvert. The *Stamford Mercury* reported that it was the fifth similar robbery within the last few months. On 19th September, 1845 Mr William Kent was the victim when 60 pounds of black and 20 pounds of green tea were stolen from his warehouse.[43]

Writing about the town as he knew it when a boy in 1840, R. Jalland a

Horncastle Medical Practitioner stated:[44]

> There was generally war between the boys and bargemen on the river. In those days the canal was the only highway of commerce between the town and the world outside, and the south basin near the (Grammar) school at the bottom of Church Lane was usually crowded with coal barges. These were often so closely packed together that it was a popular amusement among the boys to cross the canal from one barge to another, in spite of the opposition offered by the boatmen. It sometimes happened that a boy would be caught in the act, when he was sure to get a good beating with a rope's end, and be well blackened with coal dust by his captor. Those who have never known the canal otherwise than it is now (1894) can form little idea of the picturesque aspect of the river at that time (1840), and the bustle and life and movement to be seen there during the lading and unlading of the barges from day to day. A large trade was carried on, which yielded handsome dividends in the canal shareholders, and afforded employment to a number of men in the town, who assisted the boatmen with their work.

The first 50 years in the life of the canal must have been full of interest and satisfaction to shareholders and members of the committee. The associated prosperity of the town and canal moved steadily forward.

The original shareholders under the Act of 1792 (of which there were 266) who had purchased extra shares under the Act of 1800 were paid dividends at a higher rate. Up to 1812 profits were used to pay back the money loaned by Lord Fortescue and Sir Joseph Banks. In 1813 trading showed a credit balance of £982 4s. 9½d. and a first dividend of 5 per cent was paid to shareholders. Dividends continued to be paid as follows:[45]

1802–1812	Nil
1813–1839	5 per cent
1840–1844	7 & 5 per cent
1845–1849	7 & 5 per cent
1850–1854	6 & 5 per cent
1855	5 per cent
1856	1½ per cent
1857	2½ per cent
1858–1859	2 per cent
1860–1864	3 per cent
1865–1869	1 per cent
1870–1873	1½ per cent

A complete list of shareholders, together with amounts invested and their subsequent assignments has survived, and is in the Lincolnshire Archives Office.[46] Share Certificate No. 1 was issued to Daniel Allenby of Horncastle a tanner whose tanyard was in Far Street (now West Street) backing on to the loop of the canal leading to the North Basin. The William Hurst Simpson who owned share certificate No. 244 was a Linen Mercer and Draper.

The sudden drop in dividend in 1856 was the result of a completely new and unforeseen development in the life of the canal, which will be reviewed in the next chapter.

Before closing this chapter it should be mentioned that construction of the canal also increased trade and employment in the villages of Tattershall, Coningby and Kirkby-on-Bain, and for a time must have affected Dalderby when it was head of the canal. In *White's Lincolnshire* of 1856 the entry for Tattershall stated 'Trade has improved since the River Bain was made navigable'. For instance in Tattershall William Short was in business as a Brewer, Maltster and Corn Merchant. Robert Tooley had set up as a Wool Buyer and Artifical Manure Merchant. And in Coningsby Henry Hutton was in business as an Oil & Cattle Cake Dealer. All used the canal as a means of transport.

Toll sheets show there was also local trade up and down the canal between the villages. Coal was often sold on the bank from barges, and steam packets picked up and dropped passengers at points near villages. Barges conveyed sand and gravel to villages for building purposes and road repairs from pits at Kirkby-on-Bain which are still in use. Timber was picked up at Haltham from the Tumby Estate, and ale and spirits dropped off near Tumby Swan Inn, which in the 1870s had its own small wharf.

The canal not only affected trade, but was a social thread running through the countryside. It offered an additional means of travel, and was also a source of interest and topic of conversation in the villages along its banks. The men working the vessels would bring news from Lincoln, Boston, and further afield from places such as Derbyshire, Wakefield, Goole, Hull and even London. Doubtless the locks would be a place to visit and enjoy gossip. Pleasure trips on steam packets from Horncastle were arranged, and passengers would be picked up from the towpaths near villages. The canal and its traffic would offer daily interest to the country people, and quicken life all along its course.

Although swimming and fishing in the canal were activities banned by the Navigation Company, we know from J.C. Walter's *History of Horncastle* that the Grammar School boys used to swim in and near Thornton Lock, and Walter himself claimed to have jumped the lock on one occasion. To allow for sufficient room for take-off and landing safely would have needed a jump of at least 17 feet — not impossible, but nearing AAA standards in the 1830s!

There can be little doubt that most of the village boys along the course of the canal would have their first bathing and swimming lessons in its waters, where many a home-made hook, and worm would have been cast, and numerous free rides enjoyed on the barges.

The canal also spawned a number of public houses and beerhouses in Horncastle and along the length of the waterway, which adopted relative names:

In Horncastle (only the Ship Inn is still in business)

The Ship Inn	In the Bull Ring near South Basin of canal
The Woolpack	In North Street
The Fleece	In the Bull ring — later an Off-Licence
Hope & Anchor	Foundry Street
Jolly Sailor	North Street
Clipper Inn	In St Lawrence Street near North Basin of canal — a notorious haunt of prostitutes.

Dogdyke

Packet Inn	Adjacent to old coal wharf and railway yards (now dismantled). The Inn is still in business.

Chapter Seven
The Struggle for Survival

In 1848 the Great Northern Railway Company constructed a line from Lincoln to Boston, a fact which at the time did not appear to be of any great significance or concern to the Horncastle Navigation Company, which did not oppose the Railway Bill in Parliament.

The canal at that time was a successful undertaking, and had since 1813 paid good annual dividends to shareholders. In 1851–2–3 the canal carried an average of 9,710 tons of coal into Horncastle each year, and canal traffic out of Horncastle averaged 5,420 tons of corn, wool, general goods, large packages etc. Thus an average of 15,130 tons of goods were carried annually by the canal immediately before the Kirkstead–Horncastle railway line was built.[47]

In 1851 the Great Northern Railway Company built a coal wharf and warehouse at Dogdyke situated near the entrance to the canal, where coal and other goods from Lincoln and Boston were off-loaded from the trains, transferred to barges and carried up the canal to Horncastle. This increase in canal traffic and income from resultant tolls from the railway lulled the canal company into a false sense of security. In 1852 the railway company paid £1,677 in canal tolls, but that windfall was very short lived as the Annual Report for 1853 revealed:

> Although during the past year the receipt of tolls on other articles has gradually increased, your Committee have to regret a considerable falling off in coals arising principally from the supply sent by the Great Northern Railway Company being 220 tons less than last year.

In 1853 the amount paid in tolls by the railway company for canal carriage was down to £1,254.[48]

A dividend was, however, declared of 6 per cent and 5 per cent. The report confirms that in 1853 the canal was a successful enterprise with traffic generally increasing. The railway used George Gilliatt's boats to carry their traffic to Horncastle from Dogdyke, a very useful contract to him.

In that year, however, a number of influential local people including the member of Parliament for Horncastle J.B. Stanhope Esq., of Revesby Abbey, sponsored a Parliamentary Bill for construction of a branch line from Kirkstead Junction on the Boston–Lincoln line, through Woodhall Spa to Horncastle. What the canal company must have found particularly hard to swallow was the fact that amongst the sponsors of the branch line were the Reverend John Dymoke and Sir Henry Dymoke, both of whom had been presidents of the canal company.

The Railway Bill was on this occasion opposed by the canal company, but with no success, and the Horncastle–Kirkstead line was completed and opened in 1854. The Horncastle Navigation Company had opposed the Bill with real vigour according to a report in the *Lincolnshire Chronicle*:[49]

> The Horncastle Railway Bill was passed by Parliament after a protracted contest of four days with the Navigation Company and certain landowners and tradesmen in a Select Committee of the House of Commons. No compensation was awarded to the Canal Company.

Opposition had also taken place locally in the form of broadsheets and letters to newspapers by canal supporters, who questioned the profits which the promoters of the railway suggested would be realised. The railway scheme was referred to as a 'bubble', and as a means of obtaining money by false pretences (see copies of broadsheets). The railway company replied to these allegations with broadsheets of their own, and one which was issued on 21st November, 1853 was as large in size as a modern newspaper.[50]

The first obvious effect of the opening of the new line was a sharp drop in passenger traffic on the Packets on both the River Witham and the Horncastle Canal, the railway company charging passengers a halfpenny a mile only. In 1855 the canal company reduced tolls in an effort to compete with the railway, and as will be seen from the following table of tolls the traffic only gradually reduced after the railway started operating, and there was not an immediate disastrous decline.

Year	Tolls			
1859	£896	0s.	7	d.
1860	£854	15s.	11	d.
1863	£846	14s.	1	d.
1868	£484	13s.	2	d.
1869	£334	6s.	8	d.
1873	£257	17s.	2	d.
1877	£287	14s.	4	d.
1879	£148	0s.	7½d.	

The year 1855 was particularly unfortunate for the canal company because the winter was exceptionally severe, and in December the canal was frozen over with traffic completely stopped. Thus a golden opportunity presented itself for the railway to step in with coal deliveries, and they did not miss it![51]

The gradual reduction in traffic both up and down the canal not only resulted in reduced tolls, but also in reduced income for storage of grain, wool and other goods in the company's own warehouses. The wharfage fees they charged were:

One penny per quarter for first week
One halfpenny per quarter per week afterwards

A further problem was the constant friction between the canal company and Horncastle Vestry, and (after 1866) the Local Board of Health, about the condition of the two canal basins. The following entries from the Stamford Mercury are typical of many:[52]

Horncastle Navigation.
The south basin of the Horncastle Navigation is again in an abominable state; it seems to be the receptacle for all the dead pigs, sheep, dogs, etc., of the town which, instead of being buried in a manure hill or in the earth, are cast into the Navigation, to pollute the air of the surrounding districts with their exhalations. At the present time the dead body of a sheep lies in the south basin quite in the heart of the town; the pent up gases from which have burst the body (which has sunk) leaving the entrails floating on the surface. It is high time the authorities of the Navigation Company, or the parish put a stop to this filthy practice.

Seventeen years later there were still compaints of the same nature:[53]

> Horncastle Navigation.
> The River Waring at the present time presents the appearance of one vast seething cauldron of inky fluid and the exhalations which arise there are positively sickening.

The fundamental cause, apart from the filthy habits of the inhabitants, was that the two rivers Bain and Waring during any dry spell could not send down sufficient water to operate the canal properly or to flush the watercourses clean, thus silting up took place which still further obstructed the flow of water. It was, of course, quite unfair to blame the canal company when the cause of the problems quoted in the newspapers was townspeople using the canal basins as refuse dumps. Indeed, the canal company had cause to complain that the Parish Constables should have taken action against the offenders.

It would be quite wrong to believe, as has sometimes been suggested, that the coming of the railway to Horncastle brought about an immediate collapse of the canal as a viable means of transport. This was definitely not the case. In 1865, ten years after the opening of the rail link, the following goods were still being carried regularly up and down the canal, and a new wool warehouse had been erected on the canal side in Bridge Street.[54]

Goods down the canal from Horncastle	*Goods up the canal from Lincoln and Boston*
Ale (to Lincoln)	Slate
Malt (for London)	Coal
Wheat (to Lincoln)	Coke
Barley (to Lincoln)	Peas
Oats (to Lincoln)	Timber
Wool (to Boston)	Guano
Gravel (to Anton's Gout)	Feed Cake
Pantiles (to Coningsby)	Bones
Sheep	Sheep

From Coningsby Gas Works

Regular loads of Gas Water to Boston.*

From Kirkby-on-Bain

Gravel and Sand (to Lincoln, Boston, Coningsby and Tattershall)

From Haltham

Estate timber to Newark

* Gas Water was a waste product from the Gas Works, a thick black liquid used in the manufacture of fertilisers. It was rich in ammonia.

Although struggling financially, the canal operated for much longer than has been suggested by some writers. The man responsible for the final efforts for survival was the then Secretary of the Navigation Company, Mr Robert Toynbee of the firm of Lincoln Solicitors, Toynbee, Larkins and Evans. He

A genuine 'Number One': a sloop (with mast lowered) which regularly carried coal from Goole to Coningsby. The vessel was owned by William Laythorpe of Coningsby a coal dealer, who is shown on the right near the tiller with his wife (seated on his right). His son Samuel Laythorpe who carried on the business is holding the horse. Note the cabin chimney still intact, and the 'cob boat' moored near the stern. The type of horse harness is clearly seen. The wharf was at the rear of the Bull Inn, the roof of which can be seen on the left.

The vessel sailed from Goole, down the River Trent to Torksey, then along the Fossdyke Canal to Lincoln, on through the Brayford and 'Glory Hole' under High Bridge to the River Witham down to the entrance to the Horncastle Canal. When it reached there the sail and mast were lowered, and the vessel was towed by horse to Coningsby.

It was the last vessel to carry coal regularly on the canal, and the photograph was taken about 1910. The toll sheets for 1885/6 include relative entries.

Courtesy Mr F. Bailey of Tattershall and family

Butts (Road) Bridge. Main road bridge over the canal at Coningsby. The original bridge built by the Horncastle Navigation Company collapsed, and was rebuilt by them as above. The Navigation Company was responsible for its upkeep until 1888 when Lindsey County Council took it over because it was falling into disrepair. Then in 1960 it was swept away in a flash flood and replaced by a more modern structure.

was a genuine believer in the viability of canals as a means of transport of heavy goods, and was convinced in his own mind that the Horncastle Canal could be made to continue to operate by a further injection of capital to enable necessary repairs to be carried out. Mr Toynbee acted as unpaid Secretary and Treasurer to the Navigation Company for a number of years as a contribution towards its continued working. For the last few years Mr H. Nicholson a local merchant served with Mr Toynbee as Joint Treasurer.

In 1871 the committee reported an increase in traffic in spite of the River Witham being blocked to vessels at Bardney Lock which was under repair, and a dividend of 1½ per cent was paid in 1873, after which the shareholders received no further returns on their investments, as will be seen.

As late as 1872 Alfred Healey, a Wharfinger, had his own private cut and wharf near the Manor House, and he operated a Regular Trader boat to Boston and Lincoln. He was also a wine and spirit merchant. *White's Lincolnshire* of 1872 records W. Rainforth & Son, Brayford Head, Lincoln, boat owners, sail makers, sailcloth makers, and rope and twine makers, as operating barges on the Horncastle Canal — 'Proprietors of the Hull, Lincoln, Sleaford and Horncastle Old Established Trading Vessels'.

It can be noted from the toll sheets that pleasure boats and shooting parties were still using the canal as late as the 1880s. The canal was also used for school treats:[55]

School Treat
Children numbering about 430 were taken to Dalderby in boats kindly lent by Mr Healey.

The canal was still being used in 1886 for pleasure cruises as the following extract from the *Horncastle News* of 4th September, 1886 shows:

A PLEASANT TRIP BY WATER.
On Tuesday last Mr Stovin and a number of friends chartered for the day the *Royal George* and made a voyage on the Navigation from Horncastle to Tattershall and back. We need scarcely say that it was a pleasant trip, the weather being fine and everything in favour of the excursionists.

The *Royal George* was a boat about 15 ft long with a single mast and split sail. Mr Stovin kept an eating house in the Bull Ring.

It would appear from the following notice put up in the town and at the locks that activities of a less pleasant nature took place:

Horncastle Navigation
Caution
Whereas as of late years SWANS on the Horncastle Navigation have been disturbed and the Eggs stolen during the breeding season.
ANY PERSON discovered molesting them or taking their eggs after this notice will be prosecuted as the Law directs.
PENALTY for stealing each Egg five shillings.
BY ORDER Wm A. RAYSON, Treasurer.
February 1874.

By 1875 the small number of vessels using the canal meant that the Dry Dock was no longer used, and the Navigation Company sold it to the

TO THE PROVISIONAL COMMITTEE OF THE HORNCASTLE AND KIRKSTEAD
JUNCTION RAILWAY.

GENTLEMEN,

I cannot refrain from calling your attention to a Paragraph in the Stamford Mercury of this week, stating (from authority of course) that a Preference Stock of £16,000 is to be created, or as the prime author of this Scheme has it, £16,000 *is to be borrowed*. Now if this is allowed you may say good bye to your prospect of a dividend, and who would take a Share in any Line where a Third of the money has the Preference of Interest over the original Stock.

The Prospectus you have issued is full of assumptions but very meagre in facts and figures. I will supply a few—you state that owing to the easy nature of the gradients, and the liberality of the landowners, the Line will be inexpensive, how does this remark agree with your altering the course of your Line this week, since your prospectus was issued, to avoid Sir Joseph Hawley's land, and consequent opposition to a much more expensive one, where two deep cuttings and an embankment extra will be required, and the landowners quite as averse to your coming over them as Sir Joseph Hawley is? The fact is Sir Henry Dymoke and Mr. Stanhope are the only two landowners who are favourable, and Mr. Stanhope has but two acres that you will require—more than one-third of the Line will be opposed, all of it rich good land. Your prospectus gives no estimate of the amount of Traffic likely to be realized—but states broadly that the *existing Traffic* will return 5 per cent after paying all outgoings. I will endeavour to enlighten you and the public on that point.

The import of Coal into Horncastle for 1850, 1851, and 1852 averages 9710 tons per annum, the import and export of Corn, Wool, Goods, heavy Packages, &c., &c. is 5420 tons per annum, making altogether 15,130 tons—the above is at present carried on the Canal, and I think I shall be considered very moderate if I calculate that half of the above, will be continued on the Canal, leaving 7565 tons for your Rail. I have taken pains to make out what number of Passengers leave for Kirkstead and return daily, and on an average of a whole week, I find the daily number to be fourteen, or eighty-four per week—your Income gentlemen is likely to be as follows:—

	£.	s.	d.
7565 Tons at one shilling, (eleven-pence it is reported to be), ...	378	5	0
84 Passengers at one shilling each, average of First, Second, and Third Class,— 4368 yearly at one shilling	218	4	0
Extra Passengers and Fares, &c., say 500 at one shilling, ...	25	0	0
Small Parcels, Cattle, &c., say	75	0	0
	696	9	0
Half to Great Northern, as per contract, ...	348	4	6
This leaves you a splendid Income of about	348	4	6

To pay Interest on £50,000, not enough for Salaries for your Directors; to pay 5 per cent you will require more than seven times this amount.

You state that only £1 per share will be called for until the Act is obtained, who then puts down the £24,000 into the hands of the Board of Trade, before you can move a step in the House of Commons? is this to be borrowed also? I never in all my experience heard of a scheme more like a bubble.

I remain, Gentlemen,

Yours, &c.,

12th November, 1853.   BEHIND THE SCENE.

Pamphlet issued by 'Behind the Scenes' who was a shareholder in the Horncastle Canal Company. A pamphlet was issued by the Railway Committee on 21st November, 1853 refuting all the points made by 'Behind the Scenes'.

TO THE PROVISIONAL COMMITTEE OF THE HORNCASTLE AND KIRKSTEAD JUNCTION RAILWAY.

Gentlemen,

    In reply to the letter "From behind the Scenes," I beg to call your attention to some errors in it—whether intentional or not I cannot say—in the first place there is nothing put down for the Goods at present carried overland to Kirkstead, which I understand averages nine tons per week—the Passenger traffic by Omnibus and Van, &c., I think is underrated—to be quite safe I would double what has been stated—twenty-eight instead of fourteen per day—it must have been a bad travelling week when only fourteen per day were counted. The *existing traffic* will then stand thus:—

	£.	s.	d.
7565 Tons of Coals, Corn, Heavy Goods, &c., at one shilling per ton, ..	378	5	0
168 Passengers per week—average of first, second, and third class— }	436	16	0
8736 Passengers per year, at one shilling each .. }			
Extra Passengers at Fairs, 500 at one shilling	25	0	0
Small Parcels, Cattle, &c., say	75	0	0
Mixed Goods overland to Kirkstead, 9 tons per week or 468 tons } per annum, at say three shillings per ton for eight miles .. }	70	4	0
	985	5	0
Half to Great Northern as per contract	492	12	6
This leaves you nearly £1 per cent. on £50,000.!!!	492	12	6

But to cut the ground completely from under you, I will for the sake of argument suppose an impossibility, viz. that you get the whole of the Corn, Coals, Goods, &c. carried on the Canal instead of half, as calculated above, and that the Canal is shut up and turned into fish ponds for the benefit of your two 두 dinner-loving Lawyers—your total income to divide amongst your shareholders would then be only a few pounds over £1 per cent., what then becomes of your boasting paragraph in your Prospectus, that the *existing traffic* will return £5 per cent. dividend?

Now we all know that all Railway Projectors have an undisputed licence to use a multiplier varying from four to six—in this instance, Gentlemen, your men of business have multiplied by five, which might be considered moderate in comparison with what other Railways have done, for instance—The Great Northern when their line came out promised a return £12½ per cent., and the Manchester, Sheffield, and Grimsby £17 per cent. on their capitals, now the Great Northern pay about £3, and the Manchester, Sheffield, and Grimsby nothing at all on their original Stock. No, Gentlemen, you may make up your minds you will never see a dividend of £1 per cent.

As regards the advantage this Rail will be to the Trade of Horncastle—can you for a moment suppose that its trading establishments, such as Grocers, Linendrapers, Ironmongers, Chemists, &c. are of that quality and consideration to tempt parties living at a distance, say Boston or Lincoln, to come to Horncastle by Rail to make purchases? or don't you rather think it more probable that the few independent people living in Horncastle and neighbourhood, would take advantage of the Rail to go to Boston or Lincoln, where there is most certainly a better, larger, and cheaper assortment of goods for sale, to make their purchases, instead of Horncastle? How would this benefit the trade of the town? Ask the Tradesmen of Alford, Market Raisen, or any other small Market Town how much their Rail has benefited or rather injured them? The fact is that this proposed Railway would be for the benefit of Boston and Lincoln, and the damage of the trade of Horncastle!

The Landowners have been told that this Railway will benefit their estates 5s. per acre, and in the same breath the Tenants of the same estates have been told they will make 6d. per quarter more of their corn, now if the tenants have to pay 5s. per acre more and only get 6d. per quarter extra, they must be losers on a four field system of farming, only half the farm in corn each year; how stands the case where other Railways have been made? Take the neighbourhood of the East Lincolnshire line of Railway, have rents risen there of late years? Or is it not notorious that they have been lowered, some of them considerably since that line was opened. So far from Horncastle Corn Market being damaged for want of a Railway, why, more than 2000 quarters of Corn have been sold there in 1853, than in any preceding year, as can be clearly shown by the receipts on the Canal.

Your obedient Servant,
FAIRPLAY.

The above broadsheet was obviously written by another supporter of the canal committee. The penultimate paragraph contains some sound reasoning.

TO THE PROVISIONAL COMMITTEE OF THE HORNCASTLE AND KIRKSTEAD JUNCTION RAILWAY.

Gentlemen,

In your Letter to the Stamford Papers dated November 21st you have given those particulars your Prospectus was deficient in ; we can now go to work, and money the various articles at Railway prices. And as you state your proposed Line can be made in the cheapest manner, owing to the liberality of the principal landowners, and the extremely easy nature of the gradients, and the inexpensiveness of the works generally, you will, of course, be quite content with the same rate of charges the Great Northern make,—in fact, a through charge will be made. We all know the charges on the Line from Kirkstead to London 122 miles. Your Line, Gentlemen, is to be 7½ miles, just a sixteenth part of the 122 miles, consequently your charges will be easily made out. The Great Northern carry corn and heavy articles from Kirkstead to London for 12s. 6d. per ton, and Coals is *considerably less*; but we will say 12s. 6d. per ton for the three articles named, this is 9½d. per ton for your 7½ miles. The charge for a horse from Kirkstead to London is 30s., the sixteenth part of that is 1s. 10½d. call it 2s. a horse. The cattle charge is 6d. per mile per truck of ten beasts, which gives you 4½d. each beast. The sheep charge is 5d. per mile per truck of 40, just 7s. 10d. per 100. Small parcels if under 28lbs. 1s. 6d. each from London to Kirkstead, not 1½d. each for your 7½ miles ; as some would weigh more, we will put them at 1½d. each. Carriages 6d. per mile, or 3s. 9d. each. Dogs 3d. each.

According to *your own figures*, Gentlemen, your income (existing traffic) will then stand as follows :—supposing the Canal Company *allow* you to take half their coal, corn, &c. (which of course they will prevent by reducing their charges)—

		£.	s.	d.
7565 Tons of Coals, Corn, and other Heavy Articles, as carried on the Canal, at 9½d. per ton, ...		299	9	0
200 Tons of Coals, overland from Kirkstead		7	18	0
500 Tons of Goods by Roberts' Van,—average of five different classes 32s. per ton for 122 miles at 2s.		50	0	0
657 Horses at 2s. each..		65	14	0
1164 Cattle, at 4½d.		23	10	0
7133 Sheep, at 7s. 10d. per 100, ...		27	16	0
3406 Small Parcels, each 1½d.		21	5	9
39 Carriages, at 3s. 9d.		7	16	3
283 Dogs, at 3d.		3	10	9
9000 Passengers from Horncastle per year, 1st, 2nd, & 3rd class, average, 1s.		450	0	0
9000 Passengers to ditto, ditto, ...		450	0	0
Half to Great Northern as per contract		703	9	10½
Not nearly £1½ per cent. on your capital of £50,000 ! ! ! ..		703	9	10½

In the above statement we have taken *your own figures*, but we are quite satisfied the number of Passengers is many thousands more than actually go from and to Horncastle, and the north and east of that town.

We did think of furnishing this statement without any comment, as the figures sufficiently speak for themselves to all unprejudiced persons ; but we would just remark that many have taken shares under the impression that the existing traffic will return 5 per cent on their capital, as estimated in your Prospectus ; as very little more than 1 per cent is visible, you ought to allow those parties who choose, to recal their orders for shares, or it is very little better than getting money under false pretences.

Your obedient Servants,

Nov. 30, 1853. **No. 2, BEHIND THE SCENES.**

D. CUSSONS, PRINTER, HORNCASTLE.

Further letter from 'Behind the Scenes' in reply to the pamphlet issued on 21st November, 1853 by the railway company.

Horncastle Bathing Club for the sum of £135. The Bathing Club converted it to a swimming pool, and appointed a Miss Goddard as bath attendant at a salary of five shillings per week, to be increased to six shillings when she had learned to swim! The Bathing Club sold the pool to the Horncastle Local Board of Health in 1880 for the sum of £75.[56] In 1894 it passed into ownership of Horncastle Urban District Council, and in 1974 during the local government 'disorganisation' it was transferred to East Lindsey District Council.

In 1878 the Committee appointed a well known surveyor Mr T.W. Wallis of Louth to survey the canal, and estimate the cost of cleaning out the whole length, and carrying out all necessary repairs to locks, weirs, and staunches. He reported as follows:[57]

11th July, 1878. Horncastle Navigation.
Tattershall Lock. In 1870 the River Witham was deepened and the outfall and lock pit were lowered correspondingly. Also new and larger doors were put down. The lock is substantially built of brick with stone copings.

Canal. The estimated cost of cleaning out entire canal	£1566	15s.	0d.
Estimated cost of repairing locks, weirs and staunches	£1530	13s.	0d.
	£3097	8s.	0d.
Add 15% contingencies	£ 465	0s.	0d.
Total	£3562	8s.	0d.

A contract for the work to locks and weirs was agreed with the Horncastle firm of Walter & Hensman, but they failed to complete in time. Consequently the canal was closed beyond the lock at Kirkby-on-Bain for six months with resultant loss of revenue. There was some excuse for the contractors because the weather was exceptionally bad, but disagreement over a settlement carried on for some 18 months, when a compromise was arrived at. The works, however, were never completed satisfactorily.

The Treasurer's accounts for 1879/80 showed a credit balance in hand of £538 19s. 0d. but that was not a trading profit as receipts included a mortgage on the company's Kirkby-on-Bain property, and sale of a reversionary interest for £200 on their warehouses in Horncastle. One of the main items of expenditure that year was for compensation to millers for stoppage of their watermills due to diversion of water — the cause of a constant drain on finances throughout the life of the canal.

In October 1881 it became clear even to Mr Toynbee that the remaining works recommended by Mr Wallis needed to be carried out if the canal was to continue, and a sum of £1500 would be required. Mr Toynbee drafted a letter to all shareholders setting out in detail the position of the company and the liability of shareholders. The letter was approved and signed by members of the committee and sent out with an appeal for further funds, but the response was small. Some essential repairs were carried out however, including new top doors to Haltham Lock in 1882, and the canal remained open for traffic along its entire length until 1889.

Loading a barge with wool at Dunham's Wharf, Horncastle for wool merchants Dunham & Pollexfen in 1885. The cargo was for Lincoln, thence by rail to York and Leeds. Dunham's Wharf was on the Bain Loop to the North Basin at the rear of 47 West Street. Their warehouses were in nearby Bridge Street, and the watermill at Kirkby on Bain.

Courtesy Mr R. Pearce, Pearce, Pearce of High Toynton

A coal barge passed up to Horncastle in August of 1886 with coal from Goole.[58]

> On Monday the unusual sight was witnessed of a barge laden with coals being brought up the navigation. The craft we understand belonged to a coal dealer in Coningsby. The coals were speedily sold to persons resident near to Wharf Road, and placed in their cellars at sixteen shillings per ton. The average price in the town for coals of a similar quality is twenty shillings per ton. It may probably interest local coal merchants of Horncastle to know the price at which coals are brought by barge.

It is thus clear that the canal could still convey coals considerably cheaper than the cost by rail. Unfortunately the coal merchants were not interested. In 1888 the Board of Trade was enquiring as to the position of the canal company, and Lindsey County Council in 1889 suggested the Navigation Company should take steps to abandon the canal as it was unable to maintain the road bridges over it. On 23rd September Mr R. Toynbee the Secretary of the Navigation Company wrote to the Board of Trade:

> For some years past no Committee of Management, Secretary or other officers have been officially appointed, and for all practical purposes the Horncastle Canal is a defunct undertaking.

A counsel's opinion was taken as to the legal and financial position of the company, and he advised that the undertaking should be wound up. As a consequence Kirkby Watermill which the Company had bought in 1797 for use as workshops, was sold to Mr Dunham a local wool merchant, to obtain some small amount of ready cash after repayment of the mortgage, and the winding-up process was started.

The canal undertaking was officially declared defunct as from 23rd September, 1889 by the Board of Trade (Railway Department) and so closed what had been a vital link in the development of Horncastle's growth and prosperity during the first half of the nineteenth century.[59]

The canal had been a significant factor in the social as well as commercial growth of Horncastle as a market town, much more so than the railway which came after the trade and businesses had been established.

George Gilliatt, boat owner, coal and corn dealer, manure dealer, maltster, insurance agent, and timber merchant, who used the canal a great deal in his various businesses, was also a shareholder in the Navigation Company. In a spirited defence of the canal at a meeting of Horncastle Local Board of Health, of which he was a member, he pointed out that the canal had 'made' Horncastle. Also he stated that once the railway had become established by charging low rates, it raised them to well above what canal rates had been. He also made the valid points that the railway, by cheap fares, encouraged people to shop out of town in Lincoln and Boston, and by bringing in cheap manufacturers' goods would cause the small industries in the town to disappear along with skilled jobs. An examination of the trades and crafts listed in the various editions of *White's Lincolnshire* from 1826 to 1880 shows how true his assessments were.

The accusation that the Great Northern Railway raised its charges after the rail link had become established is borne out by the action of a firm of Horncastle wool merchants, Dunham & Pollexfen, in 1885. The latter asked the GNR to reduce its rates, but without success, so they hired a barge and sent their considerable loads of 20,000 fleeces by the canal to Lincoln for onward movement from there by the Midland Railway to Leeds and York. I am indebted to Mr B. Benson-Brown of High Toynton who is related to the Dunham family for this information, and sight of a copy of the newspaper report which follows:

August 1885. Horncastle.
WOOL FAIR. Dunham & Pollexfen held their annual wool sale, when there were in attendance most of the growers whose teams brought in wool amounting in aggregate to about 20,000 fleeces of very superior quality. Large numbers of persons assembled to witness the weighing of the wool which was then conveyed by water to Lincoln and thence by the Midland Railway Company to Yorkshire.

Athough traffic along the whole stretch of the canal ceased in 1889, the lower section was still in use much later. Coal was brought by barge from Goole to the wharf of Laythorpe & Son, Coal Merchants at Coningsby until 1910. The wharf was right in the centre of the village at the bottom of Hunter's Lane just below the junction of Silver Street with High Street, thus the barges delivered coal from Goole virtually to the doorsteps of house-holders without any off and on-loading on the way. Sand and gravel also continued to be conveyed by barge from Kirkby-on-Bain until the end of the 19th century.

A Gas Light & Coke Company was formed in the village of Coningsby in 1861, and a Gas Works with its own wharf was built near Butts Bridge. The works depended on the canal for its coal, and for exporting its waste products.

Coningsby Gas Works (now demolished) was supplied with coal mainly transported by canal from Goole.

Chapter Eight
What of the Future?

Could the Horncastle Canal be re-opened as a viable undertaking? The answer must be a decided yes — for pleasure craft usage.

Canoes could at present navigate the whole length of the canal from Horncastle to Tattershall, then to the River Witham at Dogdyke, but canoeists would have to carry their craft round the locks.

The locks themselves, built largely of Derbyshire stone, are basically sound, but, of course, there are no lock doors. The drainage authority has fitted a simple guillotine gate at Thornton Lock, and this efficiently controls the level of water in the stretch back to Horncastle. That length is used by Horncastle Fishing Club.

It is surely worth investigating whether simple guillotine gates could be fitted to all locks, thus giving control of water along the length of the canal, and opening it up to pleasure craft. The locks are quite large enough for all modern pleasure cruisers, and there is already a marina and boat hire firm established on the River Witham at Dogdyke.

Horncastle Canal passes through lovely pastoral scenery along its entire length, and would prove very popular with cruising enthusiasts if re-opened. It would also bring trade and jobs to Tattershall, Coningsby and Horncastle through the tourist industry.

Many interests would, of course, be affected. What could be helpful would be a joint meeting between the Water Authority, Lincolnshire County Council, Tourist Board, East Lindsey District Council, Inland Waterways Association, Riparian Owners, and the parish councils of Horncastle, Tattershall and Coningsby, to consider the viability of re-opening the canal.

It is hoped that this survey of the historical background of the canal may act as a catalyst for its rehabilitation.

Rivals. The photograph shows a train just after it had left Horncastle station on its way to Kirkstead c.1910. The train is passing the last lock before Horncastle and the derelict lock doors can be seen. By 1954 the railway had been closed to passenger traffic and a few years later the lines were taken up. Road transport and buses had been the main cause of its abandonment.

ANNUAL TRIP
TO
TATTERSHALL.

The Members of the Horncastle Brass Band have great pleasure in announcing to the Public that they have engaged the

"HOPE"

Horncastle and Boston Packet, (Captain George Read, Master,)

FOR THE PURPOSE OF MAKING AN EXCURSION DOWN THE RIVER

On MONDAY next, July the 24th, 1854.

The Members of the Band suggest, that as this is the only pleasure Excursion from Horncastle during the year, the opportunity should not be lost by those who are anxious to escape for a few hours, the turmoil of the busy town. Tattershall is a place of great interest, especially to the Archæological enthusiast: the noble Castle, built by the Lord Treasurer Cromwell, stands unrivalled as a specimen of ancient brick-work; whilst the splendid Collegiate Church, is a striking monument of the piety of our forefathers. The voyage to Tattershall also, is not without its interesting features, the rich woodland scenery around the villages of Dalderby, Haltham, Kirkby, &c., as it developes itself at each turn of the meandering river, is too well-known to require further notice here.

The BAND will enliven the voyage by a series of the most popular music of the day. A full Quadrille Band will be in attendance at Tattershall; Nectar and Ginger Beer may be had on board; Hot water for tea, &c., will be in readiness on the beach at Tattershall throughout the day, and ample provision will be made for the votaries of cricket, skittles, quoits, &c.

☞ *The Packet will leave the South Basin of the River at* 8 *a.m. precisely.* *Fare, for the trip,* 1s. *each, Children under* 14 *years of age,* 6d.

Appendix One

Topographical Notes on the Canal

The entrance to the Gibson Cut from the River Witham is sealed off by an earth bank, and the lock has been demolished.

The lock at Dogdyke has been filled in with earth, but the watercourse can be entered direct from the River Witham at a point a few hundred yards away. The distance from there to Tattershall Sluice is approximately one mile. The sluice is adjacent to the 15th century complex of Tattershall Castle, Church, and Almshouses. A footpath from the sluice leads to the market place a few hundred yards away.

Tattershall Sluice to Coningsby Lock — distance 1·20 miles
This stretch gives attractive views across the two villages of Coningsby and Tattershall as it skirts the centre of each. A public footpath runs along the whole of the length of bank.

Coningsby Lock to Tumby Lock — distance 0·60 mile
A rural section with very attractive views. A watermill was situated adjacent to Coningsby Lock, but was demolished in the 1960s.

Tumby Lock to Fulsby Lock — distance 1·20 miles
Continuation of the rural setting. Fulsby is the site of a watermill which was a constant source of contention between the miller and Navigation Company.

Fulsby Lock to Kirkby-on-Bain — distance 1·50 miles
A section through very rural scenery leading to the eastern edge of the village, where there is a church, shop, and school, also an Inn. A large watermill was situated here, and the Navigation Company owned a large warehouse with wharf. Sand and gravel was worked nearby, and continued as a major part of barge traffic until closure of the canal.

Kirkby-on-Bain to Haltham — distance 0·60 mile
The canal passes under Red Mills bridge at this point. Footpath to Haltham crosses fields to a public house and church, with views of the distant Lincolnshire Wolds coming into view.

Haltham Lock to Roughton Lock — distance 1·0 mile
Views of Roughton village across fields to the west, with Roughton Hall the seat of Sir Peter Tapsell M.P. dominating the scene, also Roughton Church.

Roughton Lock to Dalderby Lock — distance 0·60 mile
Continuation of rural setting. Dalderby was until 1802 the terminal point of the canal, with a wharf and warehouse. Goods were then sent by road to and from Horncastle. There is a ford at this point connecting with a footpath to Roughton.

Dalderby Lock to Martin Lock — distance 0·75 mile
The canal now follows a parallel route with its rival the disused railway. The old railway track forms part of the long distance Viking Way public footpath.

Martin Lock to Thornton Lock — distance 1·0 mile
This rural section continues alongside the Viking Way, and overlooks a valley to the east.

Thornton Lock to Horncastle Lock (½ mile south of) — distance 1 mile
The canal passes under a road bridge at this point. The market town of Horncastle is now clearly visible set against a backcloth of the Wolds. Recreation ground with

swimming pool (former canal dry dock). Good mooring. The junction of the two rivers Bain and Waring takes place here, and forms a large area of water suitable for a turning point for vessels. The recreation ground is only 200 yds from the church and town centre with good shopping facilities. Horncastle is an old Roman walled site.

Horncastle Canal as part of the Waterway System

The main artery of the local waterway system is the River Witham, an ancient navigation route predating the Roman occupation. The local system really starts with the Humber, then down the tidal River Trent and the entry into the Fossdyke Canal at Torksey Lock. The Fossdyke Canal dates from Roman times, and leads into the Brayford Pool in the centre of the historic core of the City of Lincoln, where it joins the River Witham. Vessels then travelled east through the Glory Hole and on to Swamp End Lock with its guillotine top gate past huge warehouses and industrial complexes. Then on to Bardney Lock and the Marina on the old course of the Witham at Shorts Ferry near the Tyrwhitt Arms Public House; past the Bardney Sugar Beet Factory, and on to Kirkstead Bridge. From there it is only a short walk to the remains of Kirkstead Abbey and Woodhall Spa. A mile or so east from Kirkstead were the entrances into Gibson's Cut, and the Horncastle Canal a little further on at Dogdyke. The Sleaford Navigation, now being restored, joins the river at Chapel Hill. A few miles further east, below Langrick Bridge, it is possible to continue along the Witham to Boston, and also the Witham Navigable Drains at Anton's Gout. Lading Bills and tollsheets show that goods were regularly carried between Horncastle and Anton's Gout.

The Witham Navigable Drains

This group of navigable drains was designed by the engineer John Rennie in the late 18th century to drain the area of fenland north of Boston. While the navigable length of the drains varies according to the depth of water, it is still possible to visit Boston through Cowbridge Lock and along the Maud Foster Drain as far as Wide Bargate near the restored windmill in the centre of the town.

Travelling north along the Stonebridge Drain it is possible to reach Sibsey where there is a restored six-sailed windmill. Returning through Cowbridge Lock it is also possible at certain times to travel to a point beyond Frithville, not far short of New Bolingbroke.

Buttler & Mallinder Report

The present state of the canal and a detailed review of its possible restoration was reported on by Mr Mike Buttler and Mr Phil Mallinder a few years ago in a pamphlet presented to East Lindsey District Council. Their survey would prove of real value in the event of any future restoration work being undertaken. The Report has been used as a basis for the above topographical notes.

Appendix Two

Locks

The original suggestion was for the locks to be approximately 60 ft long and 14 ft 4 in. wide, with a rise of water of 6 ft only, but it was realised such locks would not take sloops and keels large enough to operate direct between Horncastle and Yorkshire and the Midlands, and this was essential if cheap coal was to be obtained.

The locks were, therefore, built with an internal length varying between 71 ft 9 in. and 75 ft 4 in., a breadth between inner walls of 15 ft, and a rise or lift of water varying between 7 ft 3 in. and 9 ft 2 in. leaving the head water when the locks were full 2 ft from the top of the lock wall. The staunches had, of course, to be redesigned accordingly.

Unfortunately after Sir Joseph Banks died his papers were dispersed in sales and gifts, some even as far away as America. I am indebted to Dr W.M. Hunt Ph.D., of Boston College for bringing to my attention detailed plans of some of the Horncastle Canal locks which are deposited in the Sutro Library, University of California, U.S.A. (uncatalogued manuscript), and supplying me with photocopies. Unfortunately the University has not given permission for these to be published, but comparing plans with the schedules of locks, they appear to be the plans used in the final construction.

The lock walls were 3 ft thick with a very slight outward slope joined by an inverted arch floor. The main frames for the gates were constructed from 10 in. × 10 in. oak posts, strengthened by 8 in. × 8 in. oak struts fastened by metal 'L' and 'T' ties of ½ in. thickness, the frames filled in by 2 in. thick planks of elm or fir.

The principle of locking is well known, but the essentials are given below for readers who have not actually worked a lock.

Assume a barge going *down* the canal from Horncastle towards Tattershall. The stretches of the canal between locks are known as pounds, and the barge approaches the first lock on a pound with a higher level of water than that in the lock. Thus the water in the lock has to be raised to the same level as the pound by opening both sets of paddles at the first gate. When the water level in the lock equals that in the pound, water will cease to flow into the lock through the paddles. Then the gates are opened and the barge enters the lock. The gates are closed behind it, and the paddles closed. Next the paddles at the other end of the lock are opened, the lock empties until the levels of the lock and lower pound are equal. The lower gates are opened, and the barge leaves the lock. The lower gates and paddles are then closed. When travelling upstream the procedure is reversed.

Coningsby Lock near site of watermill. This lock has walls built of bricks with stone copings.

Horncastle Navigation 1834.

Locks.

Length of the Lock within
Breadth of the same
Depth of Water on Table
Height of Wall above water
Depth of Water on Low Sill
Height of Water above water
Clear lift of the Lock

Bridges.

Schedule of Locks and Bridges — 1834. The canal company was responsible for the maintenance of the bridges, and it was the poor state of repair, in particular Butts Road Bridge at Coningsby, which caused the newly formed Lindsey County Council to take them over in 1888, and press for the canal to be abandoned.

Particulars.	Stainville	Dilberby	Hilkby	Fish by	Conington by	Dobson
Number of Openings	3	3	3	4	2	3
Clear width of each	10.0	5.5	0.0	6.0	5.7	0.0
Depth of Water on ditto	4.4	4.11	5.6	5.4	6.0	5.9
Depth of Doors	4.10	4.9	5.1	4.9	4.11	5.9
Breadth of Thirsk Brand	-6	-7	1.1	-11	1.4	-11
Space above Water	3.0	1.4	2.0	-9	-5	1.5
Width of Surface	—	17.0	—	—	—	60.0
Water on Surface	-1	-1	-1	-1	-1	-1

Remarks.

Water 2 inches below Weir Between 5 & 6 oClock

Low grinding Mark at 7 oClock Weir Lower 4~5 on Site

Low grinding Mark at 8 oClock Weir 4 & on Site

Water flowing 7 inches over Weir between 8 & 9 & 6

Low grinding Mark at 10 oClock Water 5.6 on Site

One additional Door at lower gate Stanch full

Water 5.4 deep with a Spla sh Board 3/4 1 Thi

size 2 inches lower than the Stanch Site

R. Harrison of Edington

RIVER WITHAM to penn Veſſels, ſeventy-eight Feet long and ſixteen Feet and an
Half wide, together with the neceſſary Abutments at each End, facing the Side next the
Stanch and River with ſimilar Aſhler work of Stone.

	£.	s.	d
TIMBER PILES 120, from 7 to 9 feet long, each meaſuring 4 feet a-piece, makes 480 feet, rated at 2s. per foot when driven down, comes to - - - - - - -	48.	0.	0
Four Planks upon the Pile heads, one next the Stanch or River, one upon thoſe in the South line of the Wall and two in the line next the Land ſide, all of them 4 inches thick, one foot broad, producing 150 Solid feet, laid down at 1s. 8d. - - - - - - -	12.	10.	0
Two Main Cills of Oak free from ſap, 25 feet long each, and 18 inches ſquare, make 120 feet at 3s. with workmanſhip, - - - - - - -	18.	0.	0
Timber for the floor of Fir 518 feet at 1s. 8d. - - - - - -	43.	3.	4
Floor Plank 2 inches thick, 317 Cubical feet at 1s. 9d. - - -	27.	14.	9
Two Teir of groved plank 3 inches thick and ſix feet long each, 288 feet ſuperficial, making 72 Cube feet, at 2s. per foot with wokmanſhip and driving, - - - - -	7.	4.	0
Two Pairs of Pointings of Oak 11 feet long, each meaſuring 16 feet a-piece, make 64 feet at 2s. 6d. with workmanſhip, - - - - - -	8.	0.	0
Aſhler ſtone work, 132 feet long, 7 feet and a half deep, to average upon the bed ſixteen inches including the wings, together making 1320 feet ſolid, and for 3 fronts produce 3960 feet, which at 1s. 9d. with workmanſhip and Lime, amounts to - - - - -	346.	10.	0
Coping 132 feet long, 3 feet broad, and one foot thick, at 1s. 9d. - - -	103.	19.	0
Backing 36 Yards long, 2.83 Yards broad, and 2.5 Yards high, at 10s. - - - -	126.	10.	0
For one Gate, Breaſt 10 feet long, Heel 9 feet, 3 Bars 10 feet each, the ſwing 20 feet long and a foot ſquare, all together making 80 feet, at 3s. per foot with workmanſhip is 12l. and for 4 Gates make	48.	0.	0
Plank for one Gate 80 feet of two inch at 4d. and for workmanſhip to each Gate 13s. 4d. making together for 4 Gates, - - - - - - -	8.	0.	0

Iron Work for Floor and Gates.

				£	s	d
105 Spikes 8 inches long for Pile heads,	60lb.					
ditto - Floor - -	260lb.					
ditto - Grove Plank - -	12lb.	} 396lb. at 5d. - - - -		8.	5.	0
ditto - Doors -	64lb.					

Iron work for the framed Part of one Gate.

				£	s	d
4 T's - -	16lb.	4 times 64lb.	} 92lb. at 4d. - -	1l.	10s.	3d.
2 L's -	14lb.	2 ditto 28lb.				
16 Screw Bolts together,		27lb.	} 56lb. at 6d. -	1l.	8s.	0d.
1 Gudgeon, 20lb. The Beel, 9lb.		29lb.				
Pot, and metal Frame for Beel of Caſt Iron,		1cwt. - -		0l.	14s.	0d.

		£	s	d
		3l.	12s.	3d.
Multiplied for four Gates, is - - - -		14.	10.	8
Tarras 4 Barrels, at 30s. - - - - - -		6.	0.	0
Superintendancy and other contingencies including the Old Lock, &c. - - -		50.	0.	0
Add for Caſt Iron Clogs, making Dams and pumping Water, - - -		40.	10.	0
		916.	16.	9
Deduct for Extra work in facing againſt the River and Stanch, if omitted, - - -		186.	9.	4
		730.	7.	5
A Further Deduction may be made, if done with Brick inſtead of Stone, - - -		90.	2.	5
		640.	5.	0

Nov. 1793.

The above estimate is for a lock at Kirkstead on the River Witham, and it is interesting
to compare the cost with the £420 per lock on Jessop's estimate. It is of a similar size,
but would need deeper piling and heavier walls in the Witham than in the River Bain.
Nevertheless, it gives an excellent idea of how locks were built, and the amount of
materials needed.

Appendix Three

The Professions and Trades of most of the Initial Shareholders

Those who lived in or near Horncastle have been traced and are listed below. (From *Universal British Directory of Trade Commerce and Manufacture* Vol. 3 pages 285–289, London 1792.)

Name	Trade or Profession
Daniel & William Allenby	Fellmongers and Tawers (Tanners)
Boyers & Harrison	Bricklayers, Builders, Joiners, Cabinet Makers & Upholsterers
William Barton	Chemist & Druggist
William Bell	Grocer
Robert Broughton	Farmer
John Bromhead	Blacksmith
John Chislett	Surgeon & Apothecary
Richard Clitherow	Attorney (Secretary to Navigation Co.)
James Conington	Fellmonger & Tanner
Hon. The Champion Dymoke	Landowner — King's Champion
Sir Joseph Banks	Landowner — Sponsor of Canal Project
Reverend John Dymoke	Clerk in Holy Orders and Landowner
Richard Ellison	Banker — Boston
William Elmhirst	Landowner
Reverend John Fretwell	Rector of Winceby
Edward Harrison	Physician — Founder of Horncastle Dispensary
Thomas Hawling	Fellmonger & Tawer
Griggs Lunn	Merchant
Phillipa Massingberd	Landowner
Elizabeth Massingberd	Landowner
Reverend William Massingberd	Rector of Ormsby — Landowner
Joseph Newbound	Linen & Woollen Draper, Mercer & Grocer
Titus Overton	Grocer
John Overton	Grocer
John Parkinson	Land Agent to Sir Joseph Banks
C. Richardson	Farmer & Woolmerchant
W.H. Simpson	Linen & Woollen Draper
Anthony Squire	Gentleman
William Walker	Ironmonger, Cutler, Brazier, Tinman and Silversmith.

In the Directory of 1792 seventeen people were listed as 'Gentry' all of whom lived in Horncastle, but perhaps surprisingly only one of those — Anthony Squire — bought shares. Their status was probably self appointed — people living on pensions or small savings. Of seven physicians living in the town in 1792 only two, namely Chislett and Harrison took up the initial issue of shares. Only one boatman, Daniel Boyers, invested in the initial issue.

The approximate percentages of the total holdings of shares under the 1792 Act amongst the various trades and professions listed above were as follows:

	Percentage of total Shareholding
Business men	12
Ministers of Religion	10
Landowners	25
Farmers & Woolmerchant	7
Attorneys	16

Most of the remaining 30 per cent of the shares were taken up by businessmen and bankers in Boston. There were no banks in Horncastle in 1792, and no doubt the conditions of investment laid down in the Bill, that shares were to cost £50 and no one could hold less than one share, would prohibit many of the smaller businessmen in Horncastle from taking up the offer.

References

Abbreviations: L.A.O. Lincolnshire Archives Office.
L.C.R.L. Lincolnshire Central Reference Library.

Major sources of reference have been:

Toynbee, Larkin & Evans Deposit in the L.A.O. — TLE.1/1/1–10, which includes the Horncastle Navigation Company Minute Books, Annual Reports, Share Book, and notes by Robert Toynbee who acted as Secretary to the Horncastle Navigation Company in its later years.
L.A.O. Tweed & Peacock Deposits.
L.A.O. Chatterton Deposits.
L.C.R.L. loose pamphlets, in particular L.386.
L.C.R.L. treatise by W.M. Hunt — 'Role of Sir Joseph Banks in The Promotion and Development of Lincolnshire Canals and Navigations'. Also 'History of Sleaford Navigation'.
For the early years newspapers have proved helpful, in particular the Lincoln, Rutland & Stamford Mercury, and the Lincolnshire Chronicle. Copies in L.C.R.L.
Spalding Gentlemans Society Archives — Banks papers.

Detailed references are given below.

1.   Georgian Lincoln by Sir Francis Hill, Oxford.
2.   L.A.O. Various Turnpike Acts.
3.   Lincolnshire Notes & Queries, W.K. Morton, Horncastle.
4.   L.A.O. Horncastle Enclosure Act & Award.
5.   History of a Wolds Village — Belchford, J.N. Clarke, Horncastle 1985.

6. *Lincoln, Rutland & Stamford Mercury* 30.3.1792 (subsequently S.M.); L.A.O. Toynbee, Larkin & Evans Deposit TLE/1/1/1–10 (subsequently T.L.E.).
7. S.M. 17.8.1792.
8. L.A.O. T.L.E. — Minute Books of the Horncastle Navigation Company T.L.E. 1/1/1,2,3,4,5,6. (Subsequently Minutes Books.)
9. ibid.
10. S.M. 5th April, 1793.
11. S.M. 5th July, 1793.
12. Spalding Gentlemans Society Archives — Banks Papers; *Horncastle Navigation Engineers* W.M. Hunt. Article in Journal of Railway & Canal Historical Association. Vol. XXV. No. 1 1979. The article by Doctor Hunt includes a penetrating study of the relationship between Sir Joseph Banks and the two engineers William Jessop and John Rennie; see also treatise by Doctor Hunt above.
13. Minute Books, L.A.O.
14. ibid.
15. Dymoke Family Papers: I am indebted to the present Champion Lt Col J.L.M. Dymoke M.B.E., D.L., for allowing me access to papers relative to the canal.
16. L.C.R.L. L386 and various sub references under that heading — (pamphlets) 9648; UP9657; UP5787; UP1186; 267; 6849; L. Horn. 627/1.
17. Minute Books, L.A.O.
18. ibid.
19. S.M. 10th September, 1802.
20. S.M. 8th October, 1802.
21. *History of Horncastle*, J.C. Walter, Horncastle 1908.
22. S.M. 5th November, 1802.
23. S.M. 9th March, 1804.
24. Minute Books, L.A.O.
25. S.M. 4th February, 1803.
26. Dymoke Family Papers.
27. Minutes Books, L.A.O.
28. S.M. 30th March, 1804.
29. S.M. 26th September, 1806.
30. S.M. 21st September, 1810.
31. S.M. 26th November, 1819.
32. *General View of Agriculture in County of Lincs.*, A. Young, 1813.
33. A similarly worded advertisement appeared in the S.M. on the 29th December, 1811.
34. S.M. 17th May, 1822.
35. Minute Books, L.A.O.
36. *Education in a Market Town — Horncastle*, J.N. Clarke, Chichester 1976.
37. S.M. 28th August, 1795.
38. S.M. 27th October, 1820.

39.   *Sketches of the Town & Soke of Horncastle*, George Weir, Horncastle 1820; *Methodism in the Countryside*, J.N. Clarke & C.L. Anderson, Horncastle 1986.

40.   See various editions of *White's Lincs. Directory* for 1826 (p. 173); 1842–1856 etc; an excellent article by R. Acton *Navigation and the Mid-Lincs. Economy* in Lincolnshire History & Archaeology Vol. 15, 1980 dealt with the effect of transport of goods by canal on the economy of East Lincolnshire.

41.   T.L.E. op.cit.

42.   *Watch & Ward in the Countryside*, J.N. Clarke, Horncastle 1982. *Lawless & Immoral*, B.J. Davey, Leicester University Press 1983.

43.   ibid.

44.   *History of Horncastle Grammar School*, R. Jalland, Horncastle 1894.

45.   Minute Books, L.A.O.

46.   T.L.E. 1/1/1–7.

47.   L.A.O. 2 TP.3/1/3–4.

48.   L.A.O. 2 TP.3.

49.   *Lincolnshire Chronicle* newspaper 7th April, 1854 and 12th October, 1855.

50.   L.A.O. 2TP.3/1/3–4.

51.   For a short account of the establishment of the railway see *The Horncastle & Woodhall Junction Railway*, A.J. Ludlam, Oxford 1985.

52.   S.M. 9th August, 1850.

53.   S.M. 8th September, 1867.

54.   L.A.O. TLE/1/10 Boat List.

55.   *Education in a Market Town — Horncastle*, J.N. Clarke.

56.   L.A.O. Horncastle Board of Health Minute Books.

57.   L.A.O. Minute Books.

58.   *Horncastle News* newspaper 21st August, 1886 and 4th September, 1886.

59.   L.A.O. T.L.E. 1/1/1–6c.

The following books contain brief notes about the Horncastle Canal, the best being that by Boyes & Russell.

Canals of Eastern England, John Boyes & Ronald Russell, Newton Abbot 1977.

Lost Canals of England & Wales, Ronald Russell, Newton Abbot, 1971.

Lincolnshire Towns & Industry 1700–1914, N.R. Wright, Lincoln 1982.

The Book of Horncastle & Woodhall Spa, D.N. Robinson, Buckingham 1983.

History of Horncastle, J.C. Walter, Horncastle, 1908.

Sketches of the Town & Soke of Horncastle, George Weir, Horncastle 1820.

Index